From Victim to Victory

Sexual Abuse Beyond Belief

By Dr. Alva Wilson

4/24/2010

Pastor Smith

Continue to
be the Blessing
you are

Love

Pastor Alva

854-123-30 75 Cell

(H) 872-688-6179

872-688-6179

FROM VICTIM TO VICTORY

Sexual Abuse
Beyond Belief

By Dr. Alva Wilson

From Victim to Victory

Sexual Abuse Beyond Belief

By Alva Wilson

Copyright @ 2005 by Alva Wilson
Requests for information should be addressed to:

Alva Wilson
P.O. Box 1196
Rowlett, TX 75030-1196
Email address: faithfulalva@peoplepc.com

Registered in The Library of Congress
Library of Congress Cataloging - in Publication Data

ISBN 1-59781-768-6
Library of Congress Number: 2006900931

All Scripture quotes unless otherwise noted are taken from The Holy Bible - King James Version.

Edited by Barbara Crossley Davis
Edited by Cynthia Turner
Cover Design by Cynthia Turner
PRINTED IN THE UNITED STATES OF AMERICA

www.xulonpress.com

TABLE OF CONTENTS

Chapter 5:
Testimonies Of Victory

Attachments

ACKNOWLEDGEMENTS

Thanks to....

To the Father, Son and Holy Ghost who dictated
and directed me to write.

My dear Mother Rev. Ann Oliver, who never lost faith in me.
She was always there when I needed her.

Transcriptions by Judy Higgs, LaKeesha Kelly-Ahiave,
Wilma Bolden, Barbara Sloane, Cynthia Turner and
Baby Sister Joni Knighton.

Dr. Mike Murdock who encouraged me to write when
I attended the Uncommon Minister's Conference in 1998.
He also gave me permission to use his quotes.

Rev. Louis and Jean Burton for their prayers,
financial support and belief in me.

Rev. Pam Carter, Woman's Corner, Inc. who was responsible for
my first printed testimony, a great help and inspiration to me.

Minister Evelyn Jordan my friend for life,
who introduced me to Barbara Sloane.

Linda Marlette for her labor of love.

Dorothy Spaulding, TV 36 Augusta,
South Carolina for the exposure on "A Night to Remember."

I would like to thank Pastor Larry and Tiz Huch of New Beginnings Church, Pastor Rod and Joni Parsley and the World Harvest Church Family and Prophet Richard W. Hayes.

Dr. T. Garrett Benjamin Jr., First Lady Beverly and Light of the World Christian Church Family

Dr. Morris Cerrullo and Mama Theresa for your prayers, votes of confidence and obedience to God concerning my destiny and ordination as an Elder under Morris Cerrullo World Evangelism.

Dedications

To my Wonderful Sons

Clarence Edward Wilson, Jr.
Anthony "Tony" Eugene Wilson

And to my Precious Daughter Jacqueline Annette Wilson-
Cranford.
You were my source of joy as I watched you grow up in the fear,
admonition and the love of our Lord.
Thank you for being so sweet and obedient.

And to my Loving Mother
Mother Ann Oliver known to many as "Mama"

Dedications

This page is being dedicated to those individuals who were financial contributors of this book in the amount of $100 or greater. I want to give thanks to God for choosing you to be a special part of my life. Without you, this book would not be what it is today.

Special Thanks to:

Dr. Mike Murdock

Jeri & Greg Mauro

Jacqueline Wilson-Cranford

Cynthia Turner

FOREWORD

If you are like most people, life is far from being full of quiet, relaxing moments. As you rush from one task to the next, it's easy to overlook what might be going on in your home and family. In this book, you will find stories of abuse and ungodliness to families that said "it will never happen to them." Don't let life ever get too busy where you lose reality with God and your home. Because while you are away, the enemy will play. Using poignant stories, Alva Wilson opens her heart to help understand this delicate subject of sexual abuse. Her honest look at this subject, reveals the keys to defeating the enemy and living a Godly life to strengthen your walk in today's busy world.

Life isn't likely to slow down, but your heart can find the quiet in the chaos to seek the things your family needs most, Jesus Christ!

Rev. Richard W. Hayes

PREFACE

It is with prayer, faith and much humility that I write of my experiences. I am sharing the information in this book for the purpose of helping humanity and giving courage to those who may have thought their case hopeless. I, too, have known hopelessness and I know what it feels like. However, my first purpose is to exhort, encourage and to give new direction with New Hope. My second purpose is to spark action where it is needed. May the hand of God reflect as a mirror on every page of this book. May God anoint all who read it and may it become a blessing to all.

As I present the truth in a practical manner, it is my sincere desire that others may receive help, inspiration and courage. This sincere desire is directed to all people, but especially the single-parent families, single people without children, boys and girls, young people who anticipate marriage and married couples with children. I wish to prevent other women and men from becoming enslaved by erroneous ideas. Mothers, fathers and children may be better educated to make wise decisions in today's world of confusion and compromise. At this time divorce and compromise are on the rampage, inflation is forcing both parents to spend many hours away from home and children in an attempt to "make ends meet" or to meet the high cost of living.

This book contains experiences and scripture verses for the prevention of negligent pitfalls. There are suggestions on how to overcome as a result of my own testimony and actual experiences as well as the testimonies of a 5-year-old girl and other women and men of various educational, cultural and religious backgrounds. It was my privilege to interview each of these individuals before compiling the information for this book.

INTRODUCTION

This scripture was given to me while sitting in a restaurant near Indianapolis, Indiana.

"THESE ARE THE WORDS THAT THE LORD SPOKE TO JEREMIAH. (2) THE LORD, THE GOD OF ISREAL, SAID: "JEREMIAH, WRITE IN A BOOK ALL THE WORDS I HAVE SPOKEN TO YOU. "

(Jeremiah 30:1,2 NCV)

In my prayer time, some months later I heard the Spirit of the Lord say to my spirit:

It was fixed in 1996
Released from heaven in 1997
All is straight in 1998
Things will go fine in 1999
I will save many in the years 2000's.

"They shall come with weeping and with supplications. I will lead them. I will cause them to walk by the rivers of waters, in a straightway in which they will not stumble."

(Jeremiah 31:9 KJV)

Because of this encounter, I realized it is time to publish the book that God has inspired me to write. I write this not as a professional writer, but as a woman of God with experiences that I wish to share. I hope it will bless, deliver, and help many other believers and non- believers in Christ to "get over it."

I was visiting a church in North Tulsa, Oklahoma on September

7, 1997, when I received a prophetic word. That prophetic word was instrumental in turning my directions. I moved back to my hometown, Waco, Texas. Waco was a place that I previously said: "I would never live again." Never say never when you are a child of God because you do not know what God is going to instruct you to do. The prophetic word that I received said: " <u>Alva, your sail is set one way, but the wind has changed. You are the VESSEL. I will guide you and bring you into port. I have seen what you have spread before me, and I looked into the innermost parts of your being. I AM THAT I AM has come down and set your sails by My Spirit: From Victim to Vessel to Victory</u>."

At this time, I had just graduated from Indian Wesleyan University, and I was heading for a promising career with four doctors. I planned to be a Spirit-filled Drug Addiction Counselor while pursuing Masters and Doctorate's Degree in Divinity. However, the Lord spoke and directed me to Tulsa, Oklahoma before starting the new counseling position. Why would He say for me to do this? Later, I realized that on my new job I would not have time to take off for unfinished business, which were published materials stored in Tulsa. I arrived in Tulsa that Sunday prior to the Labor Day Holiday. On Labor Day, I received another prophetic word that said: "The prophecy in paintings are good, but there is something old that needs to be purged from the inventory. God has it tucked away until a certain time *(an appointed time)*. He will release it and force it out of storage at the right time."

Prophetess Pam Vinnett gave this prophesy on August 31 st, the morning of the accidental death of Princess Diana. Many prophecies were given that day pertaining to things to come. There was a prophetic move over the congregation. From that time forward, I began to seek the Lord for what He was going to have me do. I thought I would join Dr. King's office staff as one of the counselors, but that was not what God had in mind. He was changing my life, changing my direction, and resetting my sail to go in His direction. Consequently, I moved to Texas in October 1998.

I was sitting at my dining room table trying to write on another subject. Just then the Holy Spirit said. *"I want you to write about sexual abuse. Tell your story to the nations."*

"Alva, your sail is set one way, but the wind has changed.
You are the vessel. I will guide you and bring you into port.
I have seen what you had spread before me, and I looked
into the inner most part of your being. I AM THE I AM,
that has come down and set your sail, by my Spirit:
From Victim to Vessel to Victory."

In His Service
Dr. Alva Wilson

CHAPTER 1

SEXUAL ABUSE BEYOND BELIEF

"OH GOD, DON'T FORGET OUR CHILDREN"

"My people are destroyed for a lack of knowledge:
because thou has rejected knowledge, I will also reject thee,
that thou shall be no priest to me," seeing thou hast forgotten
the law of thy God; I will also forget thy children."
(Hosea 4:6 KJV)

Sexual Abuse Beyond Belief : How to be Healed

If you are a victim of sexual abuse or know someone who has been abused, this book is a must read. It tells the "Y. B. H." (Yes, But How) to be healed, delivered, and set free from this demonic, vicious attack and the scars left by sexual abuse.

INCEST: UNBELIEVABLE BUT REAL

My parents refused to believe that my relatives were abusing me. Therefore, they did nothing about it. How many parents are guilty of ignoring the signs of sexual abuse simply because they do not know how to handle the problem? The one you tell, usually your parents, often times do not have the courage to confront the issue or the person. Therefore, the molestation continues from one child to another from generation to generation. God called me to help bring an end to sexual abuse by telling my story. You must tell someone who believes you and will help you.

I felt betrayed and forsaken because my parents refused to listen or believe me, but rather chose to believe the boys that were abusing me. They nicknamed me "old tattle tell." That caused me to feel more shame. I had no one else to turn to but Jesus and I did, even as a little girl. The Holy Spirit became my Comforter. "When my father and my mother forsake me, then the Lord will take me up." (Psalms 27:10). He was faithful to do just that.

Statistics show alarming facts that one in every 6 boys, and one in every 3 girls are molested by the age of 18. UNBELIEVABLE!

It is difficult for one to believe that a mother would have sex with one of her own little boys (or girls). It happened to a young man that I know. There were six children in this family. His mother chose him. I don't know why. Their dad was a military man. While the father was away, serving time in the Navy the mother would have sex with her own son. As a result of this abnormal behavior, that son became addicted to drugs and alcohol. He was trying to kill the pain that was inflicted upon him by his own mother. After a series of wrong doings, being arrested, fighting and getting involved in many dysfunctional behavior patterns, he finally decided to get a grip on life. After an attempt to commit suicide, he went from being a Victim to a Victor. He decided to reach out for help and to help himself. He became a Drug and Alcohol Abuse Counselor and is presently teaching at a well-known Christian university.

Age doesn't matter. You could be 5 years old or 50, there is still hope. You can overcome sexual abuse. You too can go from victim to victory and become a vessel used by God.

In the words of Dr. Mike Murdock:

"Those who created the pain of yesterday, DO NOT control the pleasure of tomorrow."

If you are in an abusive situation. Get Out! It starts with telling someone about the abuse; someone you can trust to help you get out of the situation. Get Out!

Find a Christian Counselor, one that believes in the miraculous works of the Holy Spirit's power to deliver you, the victim. Otherwise you may not be able to set proper boundaries and workable solutions in life. Because for you, as a child, boundaries have been discarded and disregarded even before you understood the importance of setting them, and how biblical boundaries protect one's life. Setting boundaries means knowing when to say yes or when to say no. Know how to take and keep control of your own life with the help of the Holy Spirit.

Article from Waco-Tribune Herald November 3, 2002

In this article written by Janet Elliot of the Houston Chronicle, there were women in a program aided to rehabilitate female sex offenders. One women in particular discussed her sexual relationship with a 13- year old boy. She was sent to prison for a five-year sentence. She also told of molesting a 15-year old boy. She said, "If I had not been incarcerated, I might have sexually violated more children."

She was one of 15 participants in this program started by the Texas Department of Criminal Justice. The clinical director of the program had interviewed male sex offenders and found that more than half of the men were introduced to sex at an early age by an older woman. She also revealed that 90% of the sex offenders were severely traumatized in their childhood. They continued to act it out when they got their own families. Another woman prostituted her daughter for crack cocaine. Others joined their husbands or boyfriends in the abuse of their children. One woman is soon to be released. She has a grandson and cannot be left alone with him. Another one of the participants explains how she is proud of herself, she feels good inside and is *blessed* to be able to participate in her decision to speak publicly about her offense.

The women told how the program requires honesty. Admitting their guilt and talking about their problem was the beginning of the road to recovery. "NO MORE VICTIMS" is the goal they wanted to attain. Once released, as part of the program they will be tracked to monitor the effectiveness of the program.

OH GOD, DON'T FORGET OUR CHILDREN

"My people are destroyed for a lack of knowledge: because thou has rejected knowledge, I will also reject thee, that thou shall be no priest to me; seeing thou hast forgotten the law of thy God, I will also forget thy children." (Hosea 4:6 KJV)

We do not want God to forget our children. Therefore, we need to be reminded of what God said and obey His Word.

The security in the structure of the family takes its toll on American home life today. Two decades ago, North American's were faced with a new epidemic: Latch Key Children. These children were forced to come home to an empty house until mom, dad, or other family members arrived home in the late afternoon or evening from work, school, or other commitments. When this epidemic was first identified, about 15 years ago, I said, "only God knows what effect this will have on the children of tomorrow's generation, the future world leaders." These children are now into their teens and twenties, some are parents themselves. What do we see? Another epidemic: anger, murder, strife, fear, and hurting people. When I consider the murder rates in the streets and the young people killing one another, gang members coming together to do harm to others, children carrying guns, knives, and even making homemade bombs; it reminds me of what God said, *"I will also forget thy Children. " (Hosea* 4:6). Some are ready to kill at the drop of a hat. The schoolyards are a battleground as kids take lethal weapons to school out of fear, thinking someone will hurt them. Now we have witnessed the Columbine massacre, and the Fort Worth shooting: yes and there will be more if something isn't done to stop the anger. What is the cause of this problem? SIN which means missing the target. We have missed the target.

HAS GOD FORGOTTEN OUR CHILDREN?

These words of wisdom are vitally important today, just as they were when my spiritual father, Dr. Lester Sumrall, pinned them some years ago.

The World of Family (adapted from the book, <u>Seven Steps to Taking Charge of Your Life</u> by Dr. Lester Sumrall.

God ordained a family. From the beginning, He intended mankind to exercise authority in the home. The Garden of Eden was Adam's home, and he was told to dress and guard it. Adam should not have allowed Satan to enter his home. He had the authority to keep the enemy out. We have the authority to keep the devil out of our gardens. Take the name of Jesus and the sword of the Spirit and put Satan on the run every time you see his ugly head appearing. He has to flee. If you have young children or plan to have them, determine to train them up in the way they should go. God chose Abraham as the father of Israel because He knew he would teach his children the ways of righteousness.

Abraham shall surely become a great and mighty nation. For I have know him, in order that he may command his children and his household after him, that they keep the way of the Lord, to do righteousness and justice (Genesis 18:18a, 19a)

Many fine young parents today are bringing up their children from infancy on the milk of God's Word. They speak of the Lord in their homes at all times.

It's Never Too Late To Intercede For Your Child
By Dr. Lester Sumrall

Perhaps your children are older. Maybe they were into trouble before you became knowledgeable in the things of God. God's Word said that children are a blessing from the Lord. Claim that promise. Take the name of Jesus, and break the power of the devil over your children. Then claim them for Jesus Christ, and began to look at them in faith and love.

Your home is to be a haven of peace and love. Discipline yourself to walk in love there. Walk in the thirteenth chapter of 1 Corinthians and you will walk in dominion in your family life.

Christian dominion by the blood of the Lord Jesus Christ is not only meant for this life but for the world to come. The Word of God teaches that we will carry dominion into the world beyond.

Then the kingdom and dominion, and the greatness of the kingdoms under the whole heaven, shall be given to the people, the saints of the most high. His kingdom is an everlasting kingdom, and all dominions shall serve and obey Him. (Daniel, 7:27)

Kingdoms and dominion will be given to the VICTORIOUS saints. We will be kings and priests forever!

And from Jesus Christ, the faithful witness, and the first born from the dead, and the ruler over the kings of the earth. To Him who loved us and washed us from our sins in His own blood, and has made us kings and priests to His God and Father, to Him be glory in dominion forever and ever. Amen. (Revelation 5:6).

In the future life, **the victorious disciple** is to be a king and a priest. This dominion includes the material realm as well as the spiritual. Take your place of authority in every area of your life, and victory will be yours.

THE NEW SCHOOL PRAYER

Now I sit me down in school
Where praying is against the rule
For this great nation under God
Finds mention of Him very odd
If Scripture now the class recites
It violates the Bill of Rights
And anytime my head I bow
Becomes a Federal matter now
Our hair can be purple, orange or green,
That's no offense; it's a freedom scene
The law is specific, the law is precise.
Prayers spoken aloud are a serious vice
For praying in a public hall
Might offend someone with no faith at all
In silence alone we must meditate
God's name is prohibited by the state
We're allowed to cuss and dress like freaks
And pierce our noses, tongues, and cheeks
They've outlawed guns, but First the Bible.
To quote the Good Book makes me liable
We can elect a pregnant Senior Queen
And the 'unwed daddy,' our Senior King
It's "inappropriate" to teach right from wrong
We're taught that such "judgments" do not belong
We can get our condoms and birth controls
Study witchcraft, vampires, and totem poles.
But the Ten Commandments are not allowed
No word of God must reach this crowd.
It's scary here I must confess
When chaos reigns the school's a mess.
So, Lord, this silent plea I make:
Should I be shot; My soul please take!
Amen

(This poem was written by an unknown teen in Arizona)

29

CHAPTER 2

EMOTIONS, SEX,
AND SEXUAL DISEASES

Shame In The Game

You may have heard the expression **"There's no shame in my game."** There is a lifetime of shame in this game for the victim of sexual abuse. If it is not treated, a child that has been abused feels that he is at fault and that other people know about the abuse: such as teachers, church leaders and those that the child encounters. Therefore, the child is either withdrawn or will exemplify inappropriate behavior with other children, and sometimes other adults. For example, some little girls that have suffered abuse will climb upon the lap of an adult male. In a very seductive way, she will try to entice or arouse his sexuality. Her behavior is influenced by sexual abuse, loss of self-esteem and shame. She reveals a spirit of sexual abuse that hovers over her life.

"Among the most crippling of contributions to shame is sexual abuse. This causes extremely deep shame and devastates the child at the very core of her being," says Marie Powers, author of "Shame The Thief of Intimacy." She further states: "sexual sin is more violating than other kinds of behavior, because all other sin is outside the body." (I Corinthians 6:18) Sexual sin violates victims at their core.

I remember the loneliness in my own life. Being with other people was a difficult task. The feeling of guilt and shame consumed me when in the presence of others, especially at school. While walking to school with my two brothers, shame and guilt would grip me and cover me like a heavy garment. My two older brothers accompanied me to school. I recall the moment the school-house became visible, I would go into my shell. Turning my body to the side, I would take one step to my left and leaning forward, as I dropped my head in shame. I would drag my right foot along in a sideway motion, until I entered the classroom and finally made my way to my assigned seat, I could not control or stop the behavior. As shame gripped my mind, I automatically went into my shell. I thought my teachers and other students knew that I was being sexually abused and I was so ashamed. My brothers asked me "what's wrong with you?" But, I gave no answer. They also told my parents about my behavior. The boys would laugh and make fun of me. I could not explain my feelings. Now, I know I was feeling SHAME.

Flee Sexual Immorality. Every sin that a man does is outside the body, but he who commits sexual immorality sins against his own body. (1 Corinthians 6:17)

An Overview of Trends

Before the sexual revolution began in the 60' s, you may have known someone for two years and became engaged, maybe even married, before you had sex. Things have changed, but maybe not for the better.

When you put sex early in a relationship, you make courtship and dating a much more vulnerable process,' says Judith Sills, Ph.D., a clinical psychologist practicing in Philadelphia, PA. 'Most women tell me that they become emotionally attached when they take a lover. Emotional attachment makes you vulnerable.' Sex doesn't give men an automatic emotional attachment, says Dr. Sills. A woman, on the other hand who may be unsure of her feelings, will feel attached once they've had sex. It may come, as a shock when she finds out the bond is not shared.

AIDS, maybe more than anything else has changed the picture of dating in the 1990's and 2000's. 'It sets sex back about four dates,' says Dr. Sills. 'The effect is that you have sex with fewer people, because there are fewer people that you have dates with. Aside from, " possibly limiting the number of partners that you sleep with, putting off sex for a couple of dates doesn't really reduce your risk of contracting a sexually transmitted disease. Women think that sleeping with a man they've known for a few months or a year is safer than sleeping with a man they've known for an hour,' says Dr. Sills. 'It may be, but that's not necessarily true. It's the sexual contact that puts you at risk.' (Excerpts from *A Woman's Guide to Loving Lasting Relationships*). *Repercussions of Sex by Marilyn Morris April 2000.*

Jeremy was 17 years old the first time he had sex. Even though he used a condom each time, he found himself constantly worrying that the girl might come to him and say she was pregnant or that he might start showing signs of a sexually transmitted disease. It didn't take long for Jeremy to decide sex wasn't worth the worry and he broke off the relationship. <u>After a few months, Jeremy was confident he had gotten by with no repercussions</u>. He made a promise to himself that he wouldn't have sex again until he was married.

Four years later when Jeremy realized his relationship with Melanie was looking serious, he told her about his brief sexual encounter. He also told her about his decision never to have sex again until he was married. Jeremy kept that promise. On their wedding night Melanie was a virgin and Jeremy had only had one other sexual partner, but that had been several years before with no repercussions.

Six months after the wedding Jeremy was devastated when the doctor informed Melanie that the unusual bumps that were growing around her sexual area were the results of the Human Papilloma Virus- an incurable sexually transmitted disease. The bumps which were actually small warts were not the concern. It was the abnormal Pap smear which detected abnormal cells around Melanie's cervix that was the real problem. Had the doctor not caught this in the early stages, this could have been a life-threatening situation for Melanie. Fortunately, her doctor was able to perform several surgical procedures that removed both the warts and the abnormal cells.

Jeremy now knows that his brief sexual encounter that meant nothing back in high school did indeed have serious repercussions, not for himself, but for his wife. Like so many people, Jeremy ended up simply being a carrier of the sexually transmitted disease. Although he is infected and contagious, he may never have any complications himself. But because HPV is incurable, Jeremy's wife may deal with genital warts off and on for the rest of her life. She will also need to be checked annually for abnormal cells of her cervix to prevent the possible spread of cancer.

The Human Papilloma Virus (HPV) is the most common sexual transmitted disease in America. Twenty million are already infected with another five and a half million new infections occurring each year. Jeremy and Melanie's experience with HPV is typical. Some people are infected with HPV never seem to have any problems, while others experience recurring warts. Cancer for males is rare, while cancer for females is far more common. About 5,000 American women die each year from HPV associated cancer. But what about the condom Jeremy used during his first sexual encounter? Shouldn't Jeremy had expected the condom to prevent HPV? No. Condoms provide little to no protection from HPV. This virus can spread invisibly all over the genital area – the crease of the legs, the lower abdomen, and the buttocks. Condoms do not cover all of that area. With skin-to-skin contact, this highly contagious virus can easily spread from person to person. Sexual abstinence until marriage is not an easy lifestyle, but it does prevent the painful repercussions of pre-marital sex. What decisions do you hope your future spouse is making about sex? What decisions have you made?

Aim for Success, Inc. P.O. Box 5550336, Dallas, TX 75355-0336.

Sexually transmitted disease has reached an all-time high. Why? Men are disobedient to God; they have rejected knowledge. Therefore, many are perishing, dying of AIDS and other sexual diseases. As stated in Hosea 4:6, people do not believe God is who he says he is, or they do not think God will punish them for their sins.

I have heard some people say, "God created me and He made sex for me to enjoy. So, why can't I have fun with sex? He understands!!" This kind of behavior and thinking is not of God. Again, it is a lack of wisdom and understanding of who God is and what He has said. God doesn't want his people to be ignorant. That is why he gave us the written Word inspired by Holy men of God; and the five-fold ministry of apostles, teachers, evangelists, prophets, and pastors. We need to go back to the Bible.

Many are not aware of what the Bible says about sex outside of marriage. Why? Because either they do not read the Word of God to gain wisdom, knowledge, and understanding, or they read and hear the preacher/teacher speak, but they choose to ignore what is being said.

There is a breakdown in communication, which contributes to unbelief. Therefore, division comes in. Communications is the key to any good relationship with God and with one another. Talking and listening to God and each other establishes trust, clarity, and balance in interpersonal relationships.

Cohabitation Versus Marriage

Young couples today are starting families outside of wedlock because of the breakdown of moral standards. In past times, when a woman was found pregnant out of wedlock, she was shamed and found a disgrace. Now, because the standards have changed considerably, over the years, pregnant teens and women function as though expecting a baby although not marriage, is a normal process.

Pregnancies out of wedlock, cohabitations, and alternative lifestyles have become the norm in our society. It is an acceptable way of life according to man's standards, but neither God nor His Word has changed. We need to do things God's way. Many couples claim they do not want to make a commitment to marriage. Some couples have said that their relationships is better living together rather than being committed to marriage. This is a common practice among couples today, young and old alike. However, based on their personal testimonies, these lovers, are just as broken-hearted when the relationship fails as are the married couples if their marriage vows are broken. Whether couples are married or not the pain and emotional stress is devastating. Each person suffering from the loss of a relationship must come to terms with their loss or they will carry the emotional scars from broken relationship into future relationships. Therefore, it must be realized that complete healing can only take place through prayer and counseling. Since the devil is the enemy of man's soul, he works to cause people to think that they are happier and more agreeable just living together rather than being married. Some are afraid to make a commitment.

"Shacking" as some call it or living together is just another form of deception employed by the enemy to destroy God's plan for a man and a woman: MARRIAGE. So, it's reasonable to ask oneself "Why not do the right thing and go to heaven rather than do the wrong thing and end up in hell?" Some people live in hell while on earth, and then, when they die, they go to hell for eternity simply because they want to do things their own way. They choose to be disobedient to God's Word.

Marriage and family is the first institution ordained by God. *"Therefore, a man shall leave his father and mother, and shall cleave into his wife: they shall be one flesh." (Genesis 2:24 KJV)*

When a man and woman marry, they receive God's blessing. Any problems that arise can be worked out because God has His hand in the marriage. The family unit is clearly the backbone of civilization. Everything depends upon the health and survival of the family. Society must return to having healthy families. When the family is indeed a Holy family, husband and wife are committed to each other, and their children are raised in an atmosphere of prayer and order. Each family member will be stable, rooted in God's Word, and able to contribute in a positive way to society as a whole. However, when each member of the family is doing his own thing, pursuing his own desires, seeking pleasure and not following common purposes, it results in an unstable family that can quickly break apart and dissolve. If the family does not abide in the Word of God, it would be like a withered rejected branch ready to be picked up and thrown into the fire to be burned. The family as God ordained it is in serious trouble today. Satan has declared war on the family. *"Flee Sexual Immorality. Every sin a man does is outside the body, but he who commits sexual immorality sins against his own body." (1 Corinthians 6:18)*

The battle for the family is not a battle between human beings. *"For we wrestle not against flesh and blood, but against principalities, against powers, against the rulers of the darkness of this world, against spiritual wickedness in high places." (Ephesians 6:12 KJV)*

THE DECEPTION

Satan is the author of confusion: he is the accuser of the brethren and the sisters. Just as Eve was deceived in the Garden of Eden and Adam came into agreement with her, so are men and women being deceived today: believing a lie rather than the truth. "And the Lord God commanded the man saying, *"Of every tree of the garden thou mayest freely eat: But of the tree of knowledge of good and evil, thou shall not eat of it: for in the day that thou eatest there of thou shall surely die."* (Genesis 2: 16- 17 KJV)* So, what makes man think he can disobey God and live today? The Deceiver, Satan. Adam was not deceived, but the woman being deceived was in the **transgression.** (1 Timothy 2:11). He has lied again.

God's word speaks clearly on the issue of sex outside of wedlock. Fornication and adultery are sins committed against one's own body. This is not my opinion; it is the Word of God. "Flee fornication. Every sin that a man doeth is outside the body: but he that committed fornication sinneth against his own body. *Flee Sexual Immorality. Every sin that a man does is outside the body, but he who commits sexual immorality sins against his own body.* (1 Corinthians 6: 18)

In both the Old and New Testament, sex is considered natural and wholesome, but ALWAYS as a part of marriage. *"Now concerning the things where of ye wrote unto me: It is good for a man not to touch a woman. (Live in marriage) Nevertheless to avoid fornication, let every man have his own wife and let every woman have her own husband. " (I Corinthians 7: 1-2, Genesis 2:*

18-25 *KJV)*

LET US GO BACK TO THE BIBLE

Some are not aware of what the Bible says about the issues of sex outside of marriage, but many are. Why? Because either they do not read the Word of God to gain wisdom, knowledge and understanding, or they read their Bibles and hear the preachers or teachers speak, but ignore what is being said or they simply do not read the Bible.

There is absolutely a break down in communications. This contributes to confusion. Therefore, division enters into families. Communication is the key to any good relationship with God and each other. Talking and listening to God and to one another helps establish trust, clarity and balance in interpersonal relationships.

Sexually transmitted disease has reached an all-time high. Men are so disobedient to God. They have rejected knowledge. Consequently, thousands are perishing. They are dying of AIDS and other sexually transmitted diseases. Men (mankind) do not believe God's Word, nor do they think He is who He said he is; or they do not think God will judge sin one day and punishment will surely follow.

OBEDIENCE IS THE KEY

Parents, it is extremely important to teach your children the Word of God as found in the Bible, and live the example of a good and moral life in the presence of your children. CHILDREN LEARN FROM WHAT THEY SEE AND HEAR. Single parents are especially faced with the problem of living a Godly, morally clean life in the presence of their children. With the popular swinging singles philosophy "if it feels good do it," one can easily be distracted from the true purpose that God intended for marriage and sex to be enjoyed.

Some Christians are compromising and saying, "God understands because He made me to desire sexual activities." THIS IS A DECEPTION. Yes, God did make sex to be desired, but for marriage only. GOD'S DESIGN FOR THE EXPERIENCE OF WHOLESOME SEXUAL ACTIVITY IS AND ALWAYS HAS BEEN CONFINED TO THE REALM OF MARRIAGE. *Therefore, parents, especially single parents, teach your children the fear and admonition of the Lord. "Children obey your parents in the Lord for this is right." (Ephesians 6:1 KJV)* You can be that example children of today need. Therefore, they may become what God intended for them to be as adults. Teach them to live Holy by the Word of God. WILL YOU BE PART OF THE PROBLEM OR PART OF THE SOLUTION TO THE PROBLEM?

I challenge you to keep the faith. Do not allow sexual immorality to corrupt your mind! Wherefore, selfishness and unbelief will start a process of breaking down the home and family through your disobedience.

CHAPTER 3

PROFILES AND DEFINITIONS

S exual abusing a child is one of the most (if not the most) horrendous crimes committed in our society. It is becoming more frequent on an almost daily basis. Everyone needs to realize that the abuser could easily be the nice guy or girl next door, teacher, daycare worker, the clergyman or even someone in your home. When a person is murdered, they're dead. When a child is sexually molested, they live with it for the rest of their life. It never goes away.

Flee Sexual Immorality: Every sin that a man does is outside the body, but he who commits sexual immorality sins against his own body. (1 Corinthians 6:18)

One out of three females will be sexually misused in some way before they enter high school. One out of six males will be sexually misused in some manner before they enter high school. One out of five rape victims (20%) is under 12 years of age. Ten percent of all rape victims are under five years of age.

THE LAW
Texas Penal Code Sec. 22.011-Sexual Assault

A person commits an offense if the person intentionally or knowingly causes the penetration of the anus (female sex organ) of a child by any means; causes the penetration of the mouth of a child by the sexual organ of the actor, or causes the sexual organ of a child to contact or penetrate the mouth, anus, or sexual organ of another person, including the actor. This offense is a felony of the second degree, and upon conviction, is punishable by prison sentence of twenty-two years and/or a fine of not more than $10,000.

(This statute is generally used when the child victim of a sexual assault is 14-16 years of age).

PROFILE OF AN INCEST VICTIM
(This information is credited to Prevent Child Abuse of America)

Note:
- 94% of all children sex crime victims are being truthful when relating their story.
- 3% of all stories are manufactured by the child's mother.
- 3% of all stories are manufactured by the alleged victim.

1. The victim is "programmed" by the perpetrator from an early age.
2. Incest is traumatic for the victim.
3. The victim may feel like a co-conspirator.
4. The victim may become a runaway.
5. School work may drop (or increase) significantly.
6. May be severely limited to various activity participation.
7. Role reversal.
8. Pregnancy.
9. May display precocious sexual activity.

The Impact of Sexual Abuse on the Victim

Nearly always, the child acquires a profoundly disorienting, disruptive, and destructive experience.

A. Disorienting
  - Boundaries are blurred
  - Confusion
B. Disruptive
  - Attractive children may describe themselves as ugly.
  - May possess poor social skills
  - May display inappropriate seductiveness
  - May isolate themselves socially
  - May display hostility, depression, and even suicidal.

CHILD SEXUAL ABUSE

(This information is credited to Prevent Child Abuse of America)

WHAT IS CHILD SEXUAL ABUSE? Sexual abuse includes sexual intercourse and/or its deviations. This behavior may only be the last step in a worsening pattern of sexual abuse. For that reason and because of their devastating effects, exhibitionism, fondling and other sexual contact with children is also considered sexually abusive.

Generally non-touching sexual offenses include:

  - indecent exposure/exhibition
  - masturbation in front of a child
  - exposing children to pornographic material
  - deliberately exposing a child to acts of sexual intercourse

Touching sexual offenses include:

  - making a child touch an adult's sexual organs
  - fondling
  - penetration of vaginal or anus-no matter how slight- by a penis or object that does not have a medical purpose.

Sexual exploitation of a child is also an offense and can include:

- using child to film, photograph or model pornography
- engaging child or soliciting child for purposes of prostitution

WHAT SHOULD I LOOK FOR IF I SUSPECT A CHILD IS BEING SEXUALLY ABUSED?

Child sexual abuse cases can be very difficult to prove largely because cases where definite, objective evidence exists are the exception. The first indicators of sexual abuse may not be physical signs, but behavior changes or abnormalities. Unfortunately, because it is usually so difficult to accept that sexual abuse may be occurring, the adult may misinterpret the signals and feel that the child is merely being disobedient or insolent. The reaction to the disclosure of abuse then becomes disbelief and rejection to the child's statements.

The child victim may be the only witness. In that case, the child's statements may also be the only evidence that sexual abuse has occurred. In such cases, the central issue sometimes becomes "can the child's statements be trusted as true?" Some child welfare experts believe that children never lie about sexual abuse and that their statements must always be believed. However, some child welfare experts believe that children may lie about sexual abuse.

According to Douglas Besharov, it is the job of the child protective agency to make the determination as to whether or not sexual abuse has occurred; as a general rule, all doubts should be resolved in favor of making a report. A child who describes being sexually abused should be reported unless there is clear reason to disbelieve the statement. According to the American Humane statistics, only 2-8% of all reports of child sexual maltreatment are deliberately false.

(This information is credited by Prevent Child Abuse of America)

WHAT ARE EFFECTS OF CHILD SEXUAL ABUSE?

Sometimes the child maybe so traumatized by sexual abuse that years may go by before he/she is able to understand or talk about what happened. In these cases, adult victims of sexual abuse may come forward for the first time at the age of forty or fifty to divulge the horror of their experiences.

It's affects extend far beyond childhood occurrence. It robs children of their childhood, creates a loss of trust, feeling of guilt and/or self-abusive behavior. It can lead to anti-social behavior, depression, identity confusion, loss of self-esteem, and other serious emotional problems.

HOW DO I REPORT CHILD SEXUAL ABUSE?

If you suspect sexual abuse and believe a child to be in imminent danger, call the police immediately.

WHAT CAN PARENTS DO TO PROTECT THEIR CHILDREN?

They can teach children about what appropriate sexual behavior is and when to say "no" if someone tries to touch sexual parts of their bodies or in any way that makes them feel uncomfortable. Parents can observe children when they interact with others to see if they are hesitant or uncomfortable around a certain adult. Most importantly, children need to know that they can speak openly to a certain adult. Most importantly, children need to know they can speak openly to a trusted adult and they will be believed. Children who are victims of sexual abuse should always be reassured that they are not guilty for what has happened to them and should not feel ashamed.

Children most likely to be abused:

- Handicapped or retarded children

- Unwanted children
- Small preemies
- Child with "will of own" – inquisitive, demanding

Sexual Abuse:

- Physical signs of sexually transmitted disease
- Pregnancy in young girls
- Knowledgeable about sexual relations
- Reports sexual assault
- Complains of itching pain in genital area or evidence of trauma in genital area
- Suicide attempts
- Evidence of injury to the genital area
- Difficulty in sitting or walking
- Extreme fear of being along with members of the opposite sex
- Engages in sexual suggestible or promiscuous behavior
- Drawing/writing may have strong often bizarre sexual theme
- Unusual odors around genital area
- Poor peer relationships

CHAPTER 4

INFORMATION FROM PREVENT CHILD ABUSE OF TEXAS

ALCOHOL, DRUG ABUSE & CHILD ABUSE

According to the National Committee to Prevent Child Abuse's report, "Current Trends in Child Abuse Reporting & Fatalities: The Result of the 1992 Annual Fifty State Survey," substance abuse by parents or caretakers was named by 32 of the state surveyed as one of the top two presenting family problems associated with child abuse and neglect.

The lack of services for parents who are addicted to substances makes treatment and changes in parental behavior difficult. However, several states have initiatives that are allowing services to be provided to substance abusing parents who maltreat their children.

Children living in homes where their caretakers are abusing drugs or alcohol, not only are at risk of abuse, but also may experience neglect. In such environments, often the parent, will use money to buy drugs or alcohol, while the child's needs for food, clothing or shelter or medical care are not met.

SEXUAL ABUSE OF BOYS
What is it?

The Definition of sexual abuse varies among researchers and has lead to much controversy. Some characteristics that are used include the age difference between the perpetrator and the victim, existence of coercion, victim's reaction, involvement of an authority figure, existence of physical contact, and existence of penetration. Age differences can be grouped into three different categories: first, the abuser is an adult (18 years or older) and the victim is a child (under the age of 18); second, the age difference between the abuser and victim is a set number (usually 5 or more years), regardless of victim age; or third, the age difference between the accuser and victim varies with age of the victim (usually a 5 year difference if the victim is younger than 13 years, a 10 year difference if the victim is between ages of 13-16, etc.) Negative reactions from the victim (either immediately or retrospectively) about a sexual experience are sometimes used to define sexual abuse. Penetration usually refers to anal penetration of the victim or anal or vaginal penetration of the perpetrator by the child.

How much do we know about it?

Sexual abuse of boys is common, underreported, under-recognized, and under-treated. Sexual abuse of girls has been widely studied, leading to awareness of the risk factors and prevalence. Unfortunately, there have been relatively fewer studies done on sexual abuse of boys, leading to inadequate knowledge about the facts related to this topic. Some of the studies that are available have a high degree of subjectivity, poor sampling techniques, and poor designs with few control elements.

Underreporting is a result of many issues. Boys are less likely than girls to report sexual abuse because of fear, the social stigma against homosexual behavior, the desire to appear self-reliant (boys grow up believing that they should not allow themselves to be harmed or talk about painful experiences), and the concern for loss of independence. Furthermore, evidence suggest that one in every three incidents of child sexual abuse are not remembered by the adults who experienced them, and that the younger the child was at the time of the abuse, and the closer the relationship to the abuser, the more likely the child will not be able to recall the event.

How common is it?

Though rates are likely to underestimate the actual number of sexual abuse cases in boys, approximately one in six boys is sexually abused before age 16. The prevalence estimates vary widely (ranging from 4% to 76%) because of the differences in the definitions used and populations studied. This type of abuse is also related to concurrent physical abuse.

Who are the victims?

Any boy (across the socio-demographic spectrum) can be a target of sexual abuse. However, there exist factors that may place boys in a higher risk group. Boys at highest risk for sexual abuse are those younger than thirteen years of age, who are nonwhite, are of low socioeconomic status, and who are not living with their fathers. One study also suggests that disabled boys are also at increased risk. Family factors may also contribute to an increase in risk. These factors include living with only one or neither parent; parental divorce, separation, or remarriage; parental alcohol abuse; and parental criminal behavior. Sexually abused boys are also more likely than non-abused boys to have other family members who are also sexually or physically abused. Those abused by a family member are at highest risk of concurrent physical abuse.

Interestingly, there are also family factors that may decrease the risk of sexual abuse in adolescent boys. One study found that maternal education and parental concern are protective factors.

Who are the perpetrators?

Sexual abusers of boys tend to be males who are known by the victim, but unrelated to the victim. They tend to abuse the child outside the home, repeat the abuse and involve some form of penetration. But, females can also be the perpetrators (boys are more likely than girls to be abused by a female) and tend to use persuasion rather than force or the threat of force.

Threats of physical force or actual force are more common with male perpetrators and older victims.

What are the effects?

Although boys are more likely to be physically injured than girls during a sexual assault, physical signs of abuse may not exist and are usually only found within a short time period after the incident. These physical sequelae may include anal redness, abrasions, lacerations, evidence of sperm, or sexually transmitted diseases (including HIV). Boys younger than 2 years of age are most likely to have physical findings.

Silence about this type of abuse is very common. Many victims feel that they want to forget about the event, want to protect the perpetrator, and fear the reactions by those told about the abuse. Those who choose to disclose details of abuse may also find that few resources are available to provide support or few actions are taken. In one study, only 56% of these victims were referred for mental health treatment, and only half of those referred actually received care.

Negative sequelae are prevalent and may lead to boys re-enacting the abuse by abusing other children or becoming future child sexual abuser themselves. The outcomes of sexual abuse of boys can fall into three main categories: psychological distress (posttraumatic stress disorder, major depression, anxiety disorders, borderline personality disorder, antisocial personality disorder, paranoia, dissociation, somatization, bulimia, anger, aggressive behavior, poor self-image), " substance abuse, and sexually related problems (sexual dysfunction, hypersexuality, sexually aggressive behavior, and confused sexual identity) These outcomes may lead to poor school performance, running away from home, and legal trouble. Studies have indicated that sexually abused boys and girls have significantly more emotional problems, behavioral problems, and suicidal thoughts and attempts than their non-abused counterparts. In addition, it seems that the experience of sexual abuse has more severe and complex consequences for boys than for girls in respect to emotional and behavioral problems (extreme use of alcohol and drugs, aggressive/criminal behavior, poor school performance, truancy, and sexual risk taking). It was found that female adolescents tend to engage in internalizing behaviors while male adolescents engage in externalizing behaviors.

What can be done?

Increase awareness for and research in the topic of sexual abuse in boys is needed. Research is specifically needed in evaluation of victims, management strategies for the victims, and in studying women as perpetrators. Future studies should also make an effort to include better methods of obtaining sexual abuse histories, better definitions of abuse, improve sampling, more extensive data collection, and more sophisticated analyses. In addition, health care professionals should become more educated in this topic and more sensitive to the possibility of sexual abuse in their -male patients.

Therapy for the victims include reducing or preventing the negative effects from occurring, helping the victim in achieving normal development for his or her age, -and preventing further abuse from occurring or being unreported. The clinicians working with these children and adolescents may use group therapy, cognitive therapy, or behavioral techniques to help the victim come to terms with emotions, be able to manage behavior and life, and relearn acceptable behavior and normal sexual activity. It is very important for boys to reassert their masculinity and to re- channel their aggressive behavior into physically healthy activities and proper directions.

Why Our Sons Turn Violent and How We Can Save Them

James Garbarino, PhD Co- Director, Family Life Development:

For the past 25 years, I have been studying the problems of violence in the lives of children, youth, and families in homes, schools, communications, and war zones around the world. Most recently, in my role as a researcher and expert witness in youth homicide trials, I have been interviewing boys incarcerated for committing crimes of lethal violence. Boys commit more than 90% of all lethal assaults and are the predominant perpetrators of non-lethal assaults (Loeber and Farrington, 1998). As a result of my investigations, I have drawn five basic conclusions about why boys turn violent and how we can save them. These are conclusions that parents and professionals can use in their efforts to make schools and communities safer.

1. Violence prevention is everybody's business.

No matter how effective, motivated, and attentive any of us is as a parent; our children go to school with boys who are lost and who have access to lethal weapons. There are boys in every school who have developed a pattern of aggressive behavior, who have established an internal state in which they see themselves as victimized by peers and society, and whose emotions and moral judgments have become harnessed to their aggressive rage. These boys can make the transition to murder readily, if weapons are available and they reach a crisis state. Knowing how these boys reach this point and what we can do to reclaim them empowers us to reduce the odds that they will commit acts of lethal violence.

2. Children whose difficult temperament and experience put them on track for problems with aggressive behavior need help from parents and teachers to learn how to manage their behavior.

The problem of lethal youth violence usually starts with early difficulties in relationships that are linked to a combination of difficult "temperament" and negative experience. Every parent knows that children come equipped with different temperaments. Some children are easy to parent: others are very challenging. Some are so difficult that no "normal, average" parent will be able to succeed without expert professional advice and support. When it comes to developing patterns of aggression, some of the difficulties lie in being impulsive, emotionally insensitive, having a high activity level, being of less than average intelligence, and being relatively fearless.

However, these temperamental problems need not spell doom. What matters is how well the parenting and educational experiences of these children meet the challenges posed by their difficult temperaments. Of special concern are two patterns: One is a pattern of escalating conflict in the parent-child relationship, in which parent and young child get caught up in mutually coercive and aversive interactions. The other is a gradual process of emotional detachment arising when parents and teachers abandon these children by withdrawing from them in the face of their negative behavior. These patterns of response increase the odds that these vulnerable children will become increasingly frustrated and out of sync as they confront the challenges in school. In a culture like ours that legitimizes and models violence, this emotional abandonment is particularly dangerous. Once they are "lost" this way, these children tend to form into aggressive and antisocial peer groups that build negative momentum throughout childhood and into adolescence. Thus, parental education starting before children are born and continuing through their adolescence is crucial for preventing violence. In addition, teachers need special skills and a high level of motivation to create classroom environments that prevent violence.

3. Child abuse prevention is the cornerstone of preventing lethal youth violence.

The most common pathway to the pattern of aggression in young boys is for temperamentally vulnerable children to be the victims of abuse and neglect at home and, as a result, to develop a negative pattern of relating to the world in general. This maltreatment can be both physical abuse (beatings) and psychological abuse (rejection).

The negative pattern that results has four parts: (1) being hyper vigilant to the negatives (such as threatening gestures) in the social environment around them, (2) being oblivious to the positives (such as smiles), (3) developing a tendency to respond aggressively when frustrated, and (4) drawing the conclusion that aggression brings success in the world. According to research by psychologist Kenneth Dodge and his colleagues (Dodge, Pettit, and Bates, 1977), this negative pattern is the most potent link between an abused child and the development of patterns of chronically bad behavior and aggression (diagnosed by mental health professionals as " conduct disorder"). Being abused produces a sevenfold increase in the odds of developing conduct disorder. About one-third of these children with conduct disorder will eventually become violent, delinquent youths [and about 90% will go on to demonstrate some serious problem in adulthood (Loeber and Farrington,1998)]. Thus, early treatment of abused children must include efforts to change social cognitions to reframe these four foundations of aggression.

4. Detoxifying the social environment of children and youth is essential to protect them from the problem of lethal violence.

Troubled, lost boys will be as bad as the social environment around them. I have identified this as the issue of "social toxicity," the presence of social and cultural "poisons" in the world of children and youth, to which lost boys are especially susceptible. Just as asthmatic children are most affected by air pollutions, so "psychologically asthmatic" children are most affected by social toxicity.

The glorification of violence on television, in the movies, and in video games is part of this social toxicity, and it affects aggressive boys more than others. The same is true for the size of high schools. Academically marginal students are particularly affected in a negative way by being in big schools (grades 9-12, with more than 500 students). The availability of drugs and guns is another example. Mobilizing community leaders, parents, professionals, and youngsters themselves can provide a rallying point for improving the social environment.

5. At the core of the youth violence problem is a spiritual crisis.

Human beings are not simply animals with complicated brains. Rather, we are spiritual beings having a physical experience. This recognition directs our attention to the multiple spiritual crises in the lives of violent boys. They often have a sense of "meaningless-ness," in which they are cut off from a feeling that life has a higher purpose. By the same token, they often have difficulty envisioning themselves in the future. This "terminal thinking" undermines their motivation to contribute to their community and to invest their time and energy in schooling and healthy lifestyles. Finally, they often have lost confidence in the ability and motivation of the adults in their world to protect and care for them. This leads them to adopt the orientation of "juvenile vigilantism." A boy says, "If I join a gang I am 50% safe; if I don't join a gang I am 0% safe." Adults don't enter into the equation.

Non-punitive, love-oriented religion institutionalizes spiritual-ity and functions as a buffer against social pathology, according to research reviewed by psychologist Andrew Weaver. On the other hand, the shallow materialist culture in which we live undermines spirituality and exacerbates these problems. One way to deal with these issues is to have schools join with community leaders to embrace the national character education campaign, as developed, for example, by psychologist Thomas Lickona. Character education offers a strategy to mobilize community goodwill and convert it to pro-social experiences for kids. It provides a framework in which to pursue an agenda that nourishes spirituality (without invoking constitutionally insoluble issues of church and state).

Over the past 25 years, the percentage of children and youth with mental health and developmental adjustment problems serve enough to warrant professional intervention has doubled, according to the research of psychologist Tom Achenbach. The spreading problem of youth violence is related to this development. Dealing with it will require a broad-based prevention perspective on community life and a conscious effort to deal humanely and effec-tively with troubled, aggressive children, while they are still children, and before they proceed down the path to youth violence.

Perspective

This Perspective is based on the author's book Lost Boys: <u>Why Our Sons Turn Violent and How We Can Save Them</u> (New York: The Free Press, 1999)

Focus on Prevention: How, Children React to Abuse and Neglect (Used By Permission of Prevent Child Abuse America)

The PCAA publication "Foster Parenting Abused Children" provides an insight into the foster parent-child relationship and offers suggestions on caring for an abused child.

The following is an excerpt.

Research shows that, generally speaking, abused children respond to their experiences in way's that are extreme and difficult for the caretaker to handle. Although, of course, there are individual variations in behavior, some common responses have been noted.

Some children for example, become withdrawn when they are abused. They tend to hide, and they don't like to make the slightest physical or eye contact or to talk to anyone. It is as if they were not interested in people or in their environment. They don't play, they don't laugh, and they don't move around a lot. They prefer to be alone, sleeping, or simply staring blankly. They look depressed. These children sometimes act like babies, sucking their thumbs or rocking themselves. It is hard to draw them out. They may complain of stomach pains and headaches. They may also hurt themselves, by (for example) cutting or scratching themselves until they bleed. They may have trouble sleeping or have nightmares. They may also have disorders.

On the other hand, some abused children respond aggressively. They kick, bite, and punch. Instead of hurting themselves, these children hurt others, and they may destroy property. They fight constantly and are very difficult to control. They always appear to be angry. They may hurt other children, adults, or small animals.

Another response that has been observed in abused children is that they can sometimes "leave their bodies" and have "spaced out," far-away look. When these children become afraid or confused, they often are able to pretend they are not there anymore. When they are not inside their bodies, the abuse does not feel as bad. This is a very complicated psychological process called dissociation. An example of this type of behavior may be seen in the physically abused child who responds to abuse by backing into the wall. When he is leaning against the wall, he can pretend to melt into the wall, and when he is in the wall, the beating doesn't hurt anymore, because he is cold and hard like the wall.

Children who are sexually abused often talk about not being inside their bodies, but rather floating on the ceiling and looking down. This dissociation makes the experiences harder for children to remember. Along similar lines, some children who are abused can put parts of their body to sleep, so that they don't feel pain. While these responses are difficult to understand, they do occur, and it helps to know about them if one is going to try to help abused children.

Most abused children learn "lessons of abuse." One of the most common lessons is that people who love you hurt you. Children who begin to feel cared for may expect to hurt again, and this will make them feel afraid. Abused children may suffer from low self-esteem. Because they are not living at home, they may feel unwanted or unloved. These children must be given new messages about whom they are and what they have to offer. Whenever possible they should be given a chance to do things for themselves. It is important for the caretaker to reward and compliment these children for the things they do well.

Trying to help a child build positive self-esteem is not an easy task. It is important to be sensitive to the child's history while getting the point across. Emily Jean McFadden in her training packet for foster parents mentions the following four "rules" for talking to foster children so as to avoid an unwanted reaction:

1. Although you may disapprove of the child's behavior, the child is worthwhile. ("I don't like dirty hands," not" I don't

like you when you're dirty.")
2. Describe the behavior, not personal characteristics. ("You did not make your bed, not "You are a slob.")
3. Be specific. ("You took a dime," not "You stole.")
4. Differentiate between feelings and behaviors. ("It's OK to be angry, but you can't hit your brother.")

36% of Female Inmates Say The Were Abused as Children
By The Associated Press April 12, 1999

More than a third of the women in state prisons and jails say they were physically or sexually abused as children, twice the rate of child abuse reported by women overall, the Justice Department said.

The figure for male inmates, who say they suffered child abuse, while far smaller is also about double that of the overall male population, according to a study by the department's Bureau of Justice Statistics. The bureau did not say how many inmates it had surveyed, but said it had based its findings on hour-long interviews with a "nationally representative" group of inmates.

More than 36 percent of female inmates surveyed in 1996 and 1997 reported that they had been abused sexually or physically at age 17 or younger, the bureau reported. In comparison, 16 studies of child abuse in the general population found that 12 percent to 17 percent of women had been abused as children.

Among male inmates of state prisons, 14 percent say they had suffered child abuse, compared with 5 percent to 8 percent of the general male population, the bureau said. "I'm not surprised," said Eleanor Smeal, president of the Feminist Majority Foundation, a nonprofit women's rights group. "The women who end up behind bars have had a very hard life."

"Childhood abuse increases the risk that anyone, female or male, could end up in prison, because the home influence is so pervasive," Ms. Smeal said. "Women abused as children have their whole self-image changed. They believe they are bad. They end up in relationships with men who abuse them and many other risky situations."

The survey also found that rates of alcohol and drug abuse were higher among inmates who had suffered sexual or physical abuse than among those who had not.

Among state prison inmates, 80 percent of the abused women and 76 percent of the abused men had regularly used illegal drugs, compared with 65 percent of the women and 68 percent of the men who did not report having been abused.

When inmates were asked whether they had been abused at any age, not just in childhood, the percentages went up. Nearly half of the women in prison, in jailor on probation had been attacked, compared with 10 percent of the men. The survey found that a third of women in state prisons and a quarter of those in local jails said they had been raped before they were jailed. In state prisons and local jails, 3 percent of men reported that they had been raped before incarceration.

Abused state prisoners were more likely to have served time for violent crimes, the report said. Among males, 76 percent of abused inmates, but only 61 percent of those not abused, had a current or past sentence for a violent offense. Among women, 45 percent of the abused, but only 29 percent of those not abused, had served a sentence for violence.

Prisoners reported higher levels of abuse if they had grown up a least partly in foster care, if their parents had been heavy drug or alcohol users or if a family member had been imprisoned. The study noted that many foster children had been removed from homes where they were abused by parents.

More than half the female inmates who reported abuse said they had been abused by spouses or boyfriends and less than a third by parents or guardians. More than half the men who reported abuse said it had been at the hands of parents or guardians. Inmates also reported abuse by other relatives or family friends; relatively few had been abused by strangers.

Ten Ways To Help Prevent Child Abuse

I.   Be a nurturing parent.
Children need to know that they are special, loved, and

capable of following their dreams.

II. **Help a friend, neighbor or relative.**
Being a parent isn't easy. Offer a helping hand to take care of the children, then parent(s) can rest and spend time together.

III. **Help yourself.**
When the big and little problems of your everyday life pile up to the point you feel overwhelmed and out of control, take time out for yourself. Don't take it out on your kid.

IV. **If your baby cries.**
It can be frustrating to hear your baby cry. Learn what to do if your baby won't stop crying. Never shake a baby-shaking a child may result in severe injury or death.

V. **Get involved.**
Ask your community leaders, clergy, library, and schools to develop services to meet the need of healthy children and families.

VII. **Promote programs in schools.**
Teaching children, parents, and teaching prevention strategies can help to keep children safe.

VIII. **Monitor your child's television and video   viewing.**
Watching violent films and TV programs harms young children.

IX. **Volunteer at a local child abuse program.**
For more information about volunteer opportunities, call 1-800-CHILDREN.

X. **Report suspected abuse or neglect.**
If you have reason to believe a child has been or may be harmed, call you local department of children and family services or your local police department.

CHAPTER 5

TESTIMONIES OF VICTORY

The following are testimonies given by friends who have overcome previous lifestyles though their faith in Jesus Christ. Actual names have been changed.

"All who sin fall short of the Glory of God, but remember, greater is He who is in you, than he who is in the world. (Romans 3:23 KJV – paraphrased in first person).

The following are testimonies given by friends who have overcome previous lifestyles through their faith in Jesus Christ. Actual names have been changed.

RUTH – DECEIVED

Ruth lived with her boyfriend for a period of time. She begins her story by saying, "Hallelujah, I was seeking the Lord about what I should share today and the Lord told me to give my testimony." My husband and I were not married at the time. We considered ourselves as common-law married in the site of man. We lived a miserable life. We looked for love in the world and in all the wrong places. My common-law husband started looking for love in other women, and he couldn't find it there. Then he started looking for love in drugs and became addicted to crack cocaine. We were self-employed and considered middle-class people. We had nice things, self-employed, nice equipment, and basically everything we needed. We did not want for anything. One day the demons came in and literally destroyed our lives.

My husband began leaving home. Before he became addicted, he would pay bills and make sure that we had what we needed. However, when he got addicted to drugs, he started spending from $100 to $500 per day. He had legal access to that kind of money. We were in the demolition business which is the process of tearing down buildings. He would demolish a house, receive payment of $4,000 to $5,000 and I would not see him for days.

Truly, all things work together for the good of those who love God and those who are called according to his purpose.

I was not saved at the time, but there was something inside of me and I didn't know what it was. Many times, I would pick up my two-year old son and say, "We're going to go and find your daddy." We would get out of bed in the middle of the night, scouting around the streets, trying to find my common–law husband who was the father of my son. The Lord would let us find him. I truly believe God allowed us to find him.

As the years went by, I continued to believe that the Lord was with me, although I was not saved. I would kick in the door of the crack houses and say "you are going to give me my man, he's going to come out of there!" I was bold. The crack dealers would say, "Man come and get your crazy woman; she's out here kicking on the door." By this time, my son was six years old. I had left him in the car wrapped in a blanket. We could have easily been killed. I had the boldness to just kick the door and say, "you will give me my man." I praised God for keeping me safe. I believed he kept me. I could have been killed going into crack houses, kicking down doors.

Although my grandmother's prayers continued to cover me, things continued to get worse. By this time, we were not able to pay any of our bills. One evening, we were sitting in the kitchen with candles lighting the room. It was not a romantic dinner, but the candles were used because our electricity had been cut off for non-payment of the bill.

I sat there thinking, "I'm glad it's summer because if it were winter, we would all be cold." We would not have any heat. I was sitting there so miserable. My common-law husband had spent all of the money. The devil was busy beating him up because he had spent all of the money. He had not taken care of his family.

During these miserable circumstances, the Lord sent a preacher to our home to preach the gospel to us. This preacher came to talk to my husband, and explained how he could be a man, and how to be a father. That preacher was our six-year old son. Our son ministered to me and to his dad. Our son had gone to Sunday school one week earlier, and had learned about Jesus. We were sitting there miserable in our sin. Our son said, "you know Jesus, He died for us. You know Jesus loves us." He further stated, "Mom, say something." I finally responded by saying "I don't know what to say, you're saying it all." At that time, my husband got up and walked around the yard. Our six-year old son followed him while stating "You know that Jesus loves you! He loves me and I love Jesus. I want to go to church and I want my family together and I want you to stop using drugs!" Our six-year old son was prophesying to his daddy. HALLELUJAH! His dad began to listen!

I began to realize that we all reap the results when we allow the devil to influence our lives. We had employees who were also doing drugs and soon, my son began preaching to them. He said to them, "Do you know that Jesus died for our sins? Do you know the Lord loves you? You need to go to church." The employees were looking at him in awe. I was sitting at the kitchen table thinking "Woe is me." A short time later, we begin talking about going to church. The next thing I knew, we decided to go. During the alter call, my common-law husband, my son and I went to the alter together. All three of us gave our lives to the Lord. We were filled with the precious gift of the Holy Spirit with the evidence of speaking in tongues all at the same time. I thank God for his goodness.

The Lord started dealing with me concerning how we should live. I had always wanted to be married. I wanted to get married, but the devil was playing with my mind, when we got saved. My common-law husband started saying, "we need to get our lives straight, we need to go ahead and get married. Not in man's eyes, but in God's eyes." Then I said, "Oh, no one can tell us what to do. You know, I don't want anyone telling us what to do." At this time, my common-law husband started to pray and intercede for me. He knew that I had always wanted to be married. The devil had tricked me into saying "no, we don't need to get married, we are alright the way we are." We were living in sin, but we had the Holy Spirit living inside of us now. I know His Spirit was alive in us because when my common-law husband wanted to touch me, the Holy Spirit would convict me. I cannot make love with him because of our unrighteous living. I continued to say "no" in response to marriage. I didn't want anyone to tell me that I had to be married. However, the fervent prayers of a righteous man avail much. My common-law husband and the ministry of the church did not condemn me, instead they prayed and interceded for our relationship.

One day, we were in Bible study when suddenly my common-law husband said, "oh, we decided to get married." I quickly responded "oh, we did?" I finally agreed by saying "we'll go ahead and get married." Soon we had a beautiful church wedding and our son was a ring bearer.

Before I was saved, my dad and I had a bad relationship. There were things that kept us from being like father and daughter. After I was saved, things began to change. Although I came from a dysfunctional family, the Lord forgave me of my sins and I was able to forgive my dad for the things he had done to us as children.

My dad gave his life to the Lord. He died about 8 hours after I forgave and released him from the years of guilt. I forgave him for everything he had done to me. It was by God's grace that I was forgiven, and therefore, I had to forgive also. Now, my dad is in heaven.

Forgiving my dad is a true indication of the power of forgiveness. Since, I forgave my dad, my brother is now saved. He received salvation at my graduation from Bible College in May 1992. I thank God for his salvation. I believe God will perform household salvation for my entire family. I am expecting great things to happen at my next commencement exercise.

The next testimony shows how things that happen to young children often affect them for the rest of their lives. Other testimonies tell how young children are molested by pedophiles. Usually, the children are convinced not to tell what happened, and are threatened if they expose the secret. Therefore, parents I urge you to watch as well as pray about who comes in contact with and who influences your children. As a result of previous sexual molestation, many children have become promiscuous, girls become pregnant or practice lesbianism, boys become sexually active with girls, or practice homosexuality. Many molested children still struggle with these issues after becoming adults. Why? Because they are in bondage to this horrible sin, sexual abuse.

DAVID - BONDAGE AND BAGGAGE

It is a hard thing not being free. You can't do what God wants until you are free from bondage and baggage.

Hello, my name is David. In October 1988, the Lord and I met on a very personal basis. The Lord said that He loves me and has forgiven me. For 27 years, I had struggled with homosexuality because of an encounter with a relative when I was nine years old. At such a young age, I was introduced to homosexuality and that life style became more prevalent as I got older. At the age of 18, I entered college, I carried myself as a male whore by the name of Lola. My attitude was "Whatever Lola wants, Lola gets, but, not all the time." I had made the choice to live as a male prostitute, and thought I was happy. However, the Lord had other plans for me.

I quit college and began working a full-time job at a local company. Thinking that marriage would change me, I got married. Well, I was wrong. I continued to have homosexual relations on the side. The second day after our honeymoon, we went to visit my wife's family. I planned to share with them my involvement in the homosexual lifestyle. There was, however, an unexpected surprise awaiting me. My step father-in-law was a pedophiliac and a practicing homosexual. He seduced me, and we kept it a secret. This ungodly act continued repeatedly for eight long years. God had other Christians in my life. He continued to put Christians in my path. Many of them counseled with my wife and me. Then, in an effort to get away from my father-in-law, my wife, children and I disappeared for one year. God had other Christians waiting for us. They counseled with my family and me. The ministerial staff from our new church prayed for me to change. These were good, Godly people trying to help. In 1997, I was so bitterly unhappy with myself, I tried to commit suicide. My suicide attempt was unsuccessful, and seemed to make things worse.

During January 1998, my wife and I separated. She told the children about my homosexual lifestyle, I admitted to them that it was true. I was homosexual. Although admitting to the children hurt me deeply, I also felt a weight had been lifted from my shoulders. God began a process of restoring the relationship between my children and myself.

In addition to restoring the relationship with my children, He also had plans for me! I attended a local Church revival. I suddenly found myself flat on my back, so flat and so tight it seemed as though I was glued to the floor. As I laid there, a transformation started as God spoke these words: *"All have sinned and fallen short of the Glory of God, but remember, greater is He who is in you, than he who is in the world. (Romans 3:23 KJV)*

Walking a straight and narrow path is not easy. Satan always has his hand where it does not belong. Satan also has his army working hard to defeat each of us. I feel he works extra hard to defeat me. However, I walk by faith in God's word. "Finally, brethren, whatsoever things are true, whatsoever things are honest, whatsoever things are just, whatsoever things are pure, whatsoever things are lovely, whatsoever things are of good report, if there be any virtue, and if there be any praise think on these things. These things which ye have both learned and received, and heard, and seen in me, do: and the God of peace shall be with you." (Philippians 4:8-9 KJV)

"So many people don't realize what the Lord has done for them, which means that many healing and deliverance miracles remain largely UNCLAIMED." Dr. Oral Roberts.

Therefore, you must claim your deliverance and walk in it. Otherwise, you will remain in captivity.

BOBBIE – UNWILLING TO CONFRONT

"Satan's favorite entry point into your life is always through someone close to you." Dr. Mike Murdock.

I realized as I write my testimony, the root cause of dysfunctional relationships. It all started with my step-grandfather. He molested me by fondling when I was a young child. Although, he never penetrated me, the effects were just as profound. The results included a loss of self-esteem, self-respect, shame and fear.

I never told anyone. Neither my mother nor my grandmother knows to this day. I was afraid and ashamed to talk about this. I could not tell them for fear that they would not believe me and perhaps humiliate me even more. I didn't want them to experience the pain that I had suffered. Therefore, I kept it a secret because of fear.

"Getting rid of fear is going to be a tough battle. Just when you conquer one fear something else will pop up and you will be afraid again. At least that's the way it was for me for a long time," say Jan Morrison. Ms. Morrison further states that she fought the tough battle by learning the truth and repeatedly telling herself the truth. For example, if you feel that you are responsible for keeping your family together, tell yourself the truth. "I am not responsible for what happens to my family. My abuser is. He is the one that chose to put his desires above the good of the family. He is the guilty one, not me." *"I have no greater joy than to hear that my children walk in truth!" (3 John 1:4 KJV)*

I praise and thank God for allowing me to be chosen to give my testimony. I pray that it will be a blessing to many who read it. This part of my testimony begins with a boyfriend. I met him early in 1990, when I was 15 years old. For a while, we were just friends. Soon we became more than friends, and went everywhere together. He was always around me, and never stayed away from me for over an hour.

When I turned 17 years old, I became pregnant with his child. It was my first pregnancy, and my body wanted to reject the baby. I was sick all the time, so sick that I could hardly get out of bed. When I knew I was expecting a baby, I weighed 200 pounds. By the fourth month, I weighed 120 pounds. I was so sick I could not keep anything on my stomach. I could not stand up to walk. I did not have any insurance or Medicaid, there was not much the doctors could do for me. The doctor encouraged me to eat for the health of my baby.

At this time, I moved in with my by boyfriend's mother. She would not let me stay unless I attended school. I was in the eleventh grade when I enrolled, I was not held back. This was a blessing from God. Five months pregnant and re-enrolled in school, I realized that I had to do what was necessary in order to graduate. I needed to graduate not only for myself, but now I had another person, my unborn baby, to be concerned about for survival.

In late 1990, I began a high school program that would enable me to graduate five months early. Just before graduation, a teacher that was involved in the program asked me what I was going to do next. I didn't exactly know what I would do next, but I did know that I wanted to be a nurse. God blessed me once again. This teacher paid for my college entrance exam. I enrolled at a local college, and graduated as a nurse. I feel it was vitally important to have someone take interest in another person's life, and push them to full potential. I continuously thank God for that teacher who was there when I needed someone.

After giving birth to a baby girl, the relationship between the baby's father and me became strained. He and I were living together in an apartment that I had rented. He was irresponsible. He sold drugs until his arrest. He spent time in prison for his crime. I realized this relationship was fatal and I broke it off.

I began to see another man. He and my baby's father seemed to have total opposite personalities. This relationship went well for about six months, until I learned that I was pregnant again. I went into total denial as I did not want to have another baby out of wedlock, but I was pregnant.

My boyfriend became extremely possessive. Our relationship took a sharp turn for the worst. We would argue and get into physical fights. Time past and we started going to church and became Christians. After that, the fist fights ended, but the verbal arguments continued. We continued living together for the next four years.

Our pastor counseled with us and suggested that we stop living together. We believed from a Christian point-of-view that if we were married, God and man would respect our relationship. We did not realize that we had unresolved issues and getting married would not solve the problems. We continued with our plans to get married. Everything was set and we were just waiting for the big day, August 18, 1995. While sitting in church one Sunday, a dear friend whom I admire was staring at me. She was gifted in intercession and the word of knowledge (a prophetess).

As our eyes met, she blurted out "That's not for you." I said, "What?" She nodded her head toward my boyfriend. Then I looked around and my eyes fell on him. The prophetess said "God said 'He's got somebody better for you'." In my mind I said "Why, who?" I doubted what she said, and didn't want to believe it. I prayed to God for myself. I asked Him to show me if I was doing the right thing. He did.

Upon arrival at my home from Church, my boyfriend started an argument for the final time. Things escalated, and then he did something I never thought he would do again. During that time, I began to pray and thank God for what he had shown me. I ended the relationship although he tried to talk me into staying with him. God had shown me without a shadow of a doubt that I was not to marry him. I WAS OBEDIENT.

Listen to God's voice Marilyn Hickey stated, "Remember that God's hand protects your life. At times the battle may seem so intense, that you may think all is lost. God's peace will be with you even on the most stressful occasions."

"But if thou shall indeed obey his voice, and do all that I speak; then I will be an enemy unto thine enemies, and an adversary unto thine adversaries." (Exodus 23:22KJV)

I remained a single woman with three little children for sometime. My mother played a vital part in our lives. She was there for us every step of the way. We serve God together as a family at home and at church. I lived my life for God and waited for Him to send my Boaz. Abstinence was not an easy lifestyle for me, but it is possible with God's help. I learned to trust Him. I continued to give God glory for all the things He brought me through. I know God has been with me even when I did not know Him. PRAISE GOD. I was not one of the 36% of female inmates that were incarcerated due to murder of an abusive boyfriend or spouse. The Holy Spirit of God kept me from total disaster. PRAISE GOD!

Once again God has come through for me. As I have continued to serve Him and seek his face and stay committed to His work, God has sent into my life a Godly man. This is a man that loves God with all his heart, mind, and strength. He is a blessing to me and my family. I continue to trust God that He will work through us as a united couple and bless our marriage as we serve Him whole-heartedly.

CANDY-5 YEARS OLD
HOW YOUNG IS TO YOUNG

Grandma: Now, what is this you said this little boy was trying to do... Wanted you to do what now?

Candy: He wants me to suck his private, I said no. Then he went outside with no panties on, or nothing, not even a shirt.

Grandma: Where was his momma?

Candy: At work. She was at work.

Grandma: Where was the grandmother?

Candy: The grandma was in the house.

Grandma: She was in the house? How old is this little boy?

Candy: Uh, nine.

Grandma: Nine years old? And now what did you say someone was trying to do to your brother?

Candy: This girl was trying to suck my brother's private.

Grandma: Where was she when she was trying to do that?

Candy: In my brother's room.

Grandma: Where was your mamma?

Candy: She was at work.

Grandma: Where was your poppa?

Candy: Gone to take my momma to work.

Grandma: Today?

Candy: Yeah.

Grandma: You were over here, or was this before I picked you up this morning, that this girl came over?

Candy: She came over when my brother was at home and ask if she could borrow some sugar and I said yeah. Then my brother hit her in her eye and it turned brown.

Grandma: Her eye turned black?

Candy: Yeah.

Grandma: Did she get to do this thing that she was trying to do?

Candy: Yes, she was trying to suck his private

Grandma: But did she get to do it?

Candy: Yeah.

Grandma: She did it? He stood there and let her?

Candy: HHMM?

Grandma: He stood there and let her do it?

Candy: No, he hit her in the face while she was doing this. He said, "bop." (Candy motioned with her fist)

Grandma: He hit her in the face? Is this girl married? Did you say she was a grown lady?

Candy: She's not grown, I told you, "she has a husband and they live downstairs from us. Her name is Sarah.

Grandma: She came up to borrow sugar and your daddy and momma were gone?

Candy: I said, " Go get a plate or something," my mommy was gone the first time she came to get the sugar and I ask my brother to get the sugar for me. He said, "Where is the sugar" I said, "up in the thing that mommy showed you in the counter. He came up and slapped her when she tried to get underneath there and suck his private and she had already did it.

Grandma: How did you learn about that? How did you learn about people sucking?

Candy: I was in the room with them and she went on and sucked his private.

Grandma: This morning? That was this morning?

Candy: No, it was the day before it. The day before this one.

Grandma: Oh me, I think that's awful. Who told you about...where did you first hear about sucking?

Candy: She was trying to suck his private and I was in the room. I came in, I tried to hit her in the belly and my brother wacked her upside her head.

Grandma: Did you ever tell your daddy and mommy about these things?

Candy: No, I told this little girl Freda.

Grandma: Why not?

Candy: My brother told my mommy and my daddy.

Grandma: What did they say?

Candy: I don't know, I wasn't in the room. I was outside.

Grandma: Has anyone tried to do these things to you and your sister?

Candy: Yeah, Mike.

Grandma: Who is Mike?

Candy: That boy I just told you about.

Grandma: That fat boy?

Candy: Yeah.

Grandma: And what did you do when he tried?

Candy: I punched him in the face and told him to get on out when he finished.

Grandma: When he finished doing what?

Candy: He was trying to suck me and my sister. He was trying to suck our privates, he was trying to suck our butts and suck our cha-chas, and he eats hair.

Grandma: *(Grandma laughs)* It's not funny. He eats hair? How old is this little boy?

Candy: Nine.

Grandma: Tell me about this little boy. Has he ever sucked your cha-chas?
(Candy began moving up and down as if the boy was going up and down on her)
Did he lick your cha-chas and put his tongue on you?

Candy: He did my sister like this...(*Candy began to move her body as if she was making love, in and out*).

Grandma: Where did he do this?

Candy: He came up to my sister and tried to kiss her and he was doing it at the same time.

Grandma: Doing what at the same time?

Candy: Sucking my sister's private and me, and sucking my cha-chas.

Grandma: Where are your cha-chas?

Candy: Those up there. *(pointing to her breast)*

Grandma: He was sucking your breast. What else was he doing?

Candy: He came and started. *(Candy began using sexual motions with her body).*

Grandma: When he did like that did he put anything inside of you?

Candy: He put his thing inside of my sister

Grandma: And was going like that? And what did she do?

Candy: Pressed on the side of his face and made him get out of her.

Grandma: What did your sister do?

Candy: She slapped him in the face.

Grandma: Did ya'll tell any body?

Candy: I told my brother and he bust him up side his head.

Grandma: You didn't tell your mommy or your daddy? How come you didn't tell them?

Candy: Because my brother told them, he told them everything Mike did. He slammed me on the ground and his grandma said, "you shouldn't ever do that to her," and he got another whipping from her. I told my brother and he punched him upside his head and threw him up side that rail... that big rail, and he (Mike) was crying.

Grandma: I'm going to talk to your mommy and daddy and get some things straightened out for y'all, so you will not have to go through this kind of stuff. Little girls shouldn't have to go through that kind of behavior.

Candy: Can I tell you something else?

Grandma: Well, when he tried to put his private in, he couldn't put it in both of you at the same time, so what?

Candy: He put it in my sister first and then he was sucking her. Then he told her to come here, he had to tell her something. and then he pulled his thing out of his pants again and sucked her and then he kissed her.

Grandma: When he sucked her, where did he put his mouth?

Candy: On her private.

Grandma: So then, when he got through sucking your sister *(Candy interrupts)*

Candy: He did the same thing to me. My sister said come up and I said I'm coming up. He came up and he pulled his shirt up and he just had on his underwear. Then he pulled out his thing out of his underwear and came to me and licked me and kissed me on my private and then did stuff to me like he did to my sister. I punched him in his face. That's it.

Grandma: How many times has he done this to you?

Candy: Four times.

Grandma: All in the same day or another day?

Candy: Another day and another day.

Grandma: And you don't want to tell your daddy?

Candy: My brother told him. He told Mike you better get off my two sisters, before I punch you in the face, hit you up side your head and throw you down in the street and make you get ran over.

Grandma: I'm sorry that this has happened to you.

Candy: I want to stay living here.

Grandma: You want to live over here?

Candy: Yeah!

Grandma: Why do you want to live over here?

Candy: Cause it ain't no nasty boys or no nasty girls sucking their brother's thing.

Candy's Testimony

A five-year old girl represents thousands of innocent children. Victims are both boys and girls in the United States as well as other nations of which I have not done an extensive study. They are children whose cries will never be heard. Also, they will hurt and suffer silently while the rest of the world stands idly by and does nothing for them. Who will help them? Who will take responsibility to rescue them? This writing is geared toward helping helpless and hurting humanity. Its purpose is to shine a bright light on the enemy (Satan) and the evil that he perpetrates on mankind. I have found the answer: dysfunctional behavior in people who as children were never saved, delivered, healed (sozo) and set free from some type of abuse; most likely sexual abuse. They will allow their children to suffer this hideous crime. Some will abuse their own children.

I wish to thank Prevent Child Abuse of Texas (PCA) for permission to use their printed materials. Without PCA this book would have been incomplete. Their generosity is greatly appreciated. Allowing me to reprint information in my book benefits those who may not take the time to go to the library and obtain pertinent information on this subject or have the opportunity to read the facts.

Please join us in prayer as we together turn this large ship around with a very small rudder. Although there are agencies such as Child Protective Services (CPS) that are designed to help, and they do (consequently the assignments and duties are not always completed). They fall short. CPS have rescued many children at risk, I am sure. However, in the case with Candy as well as some other children at risk, they have missed the mark. Simply said, they have sinned against the children and God. Sin means to miss the mark. I must, however, point out the fact that there are some weak links within their chain (system). I hope CPS will see and identify these links and replace them with brand new strong links that cannot be broken. The enclosed letter written by a CPS caseworker is proof (see attachment). It is a sin and a shame before God for a five-year old child to be placed back into a dreadful situation as was little Candy. She had no one else to turn to.

Her grandmother was forbidden by the parents to ever visit her again. It is time someone stepped into the pathway of light and fight the good fight of faith for these helpless, hopeless children. The Church of Jesus Christ should be the ones to turn to. But, we have failed miserably. Many pastors seem to be afraid to address any sexual sin or abuse. If not you, then who? If not now, then when? I challenge you to join me in prayer for agencies such as CPS and its employees.

Pray that they will be thorough in their investigations. Pray that they will not feel overwhelmed and decide to take the easy way out. Encourage your local caseworkers by calling and asking if you can be a volunteer. Help in any way that can benefit them. Lighten the burden by working with them. A word of caution: If you are one who has experienced problems with pedophilia PLEASE do not get involved unless you personally have been TOTALLY delivered by the Blood of Jesus. As you are reading this book we are praying for YOU. Although the caseworkers may be overloaded with work, they must NOT neglect their duties. The reason for the existence of their jobs is to help children, not just to receive a paycheck.

In Candy's case, it appeared that the caseworker used intimidation to embarrass the grandmother. She wanted her to recant from her original accusation. Questions were asked in a very harsh voice "How do you know this happened?" As well as, "Why did you wait so long to report this? The caseworker said that-the grandmother had waited too long to do anything about the situation. It seems the caseworker did not want to work with the case. This is one of the main reasons that so many people do not report or seek help in sexual abuse cases. They are made the victim. In essence the caseworker implied that the grandmother made up her story simply because she_did not like Candy's mother. She felt the grandmother wanted to hurt Candy's mother which was not the truth. How foolish! In other words the caseworker seemed to accuse the grandmother of telling a lie. However Candy's grandmother had taped the voice of Candy's testimony. This was good thinking on the grandmother's part. She thought "I will present the tape unedited to CPS." She also thought this would be all the evidence needed to convince CPS, but it was not. The letter from the CPS caseworker (found at the end of this book as an attachment) is proof that this employee did not have the child's interest at heart. It was only a routine investigation. I realize that not all employees are like the aforementioned, but those who are not truly interested in the child's best interest should be reprimanded, as well as thoroughly screened before they are hired. May the Lord help us!!!!! We must go into the enemies (Satan) camp and take back every innocent boy and girl the enemy has tried to destroy. There is hope.

Together we must roll up our sleeves and work, work, work. We must shine the light of God's word into darkness. By that I mean, expose the evil that is being perpetrated on our future leaders, our children. What is our purpose? It is to put an end to sexual abuse. Sexual abuse leaves scars, mistrust, shame, guilt, and mixed up personalities. If sexual abuse is not dealt with properly, it will cause broken marriages later in life. That is just some of its many affects. Have you ever wondered why there are so many divorces, even in Christian marriages? Many times the problem stems from sexual abuse. The abuse was never addressed, but suppressed. Feelings of abandonment and other abnormalities rule over its victims.

Dysfunctional Parents and How They Affect Their Children

Many times dysfunctional parents attributed to sexual abuse because they have been sexually abused. As a result of their own abuse, they have not learned to set proper boundaries to protect their children. When the parents are on drugs or alcohol this is especially true. In the case of Candy, both parents are alleged substance abusers. Therefore, who will protect the innocent children when the parents are high? The parents are not capable. I believe this is where CPS needs to step in, however, they do not always discern or observe the substance abusive parents. As was the situation with Candy's parents, they were able to hide the evidence. Drug and alcohol users can be very deceptive at least on the surface, from the caseworker. Caseworkers must discern not by what they see or hear the parents say with their natural eye or ears but by the eyes of the Holy Spirit (discernment). In other words, the only way this is going to be resolved is by the help of the Lord. Otherwise the caseworkers will be deceived and the children will be left in an unsafe environment just as Candy was with no place to turn for help.

Candy's testimony is exactly as she spoke it except the word "private." The word private was substituted to soften the language for the reader. The grandmother, after hearing the start of Candy's story, stopped Candy from talking until she could get the tape recorder. She placed it under the table where Candy could not see it and recorded her story verbatim. In the beginning, Candy did not know she was being recorded. Grandmother was stunned by Candy's account of what she had experienced.

Later that day grandmother confronted Candy's daddy and mother with Candy's testimony. Candy's mother who was allegedly a substance abuser at that time sat and stared straight ahead with a blank look on her face as if grandmother was not talking to her. Candy's dad immediately became defensive. His reply was one of disbelief. He said, "Candy has a wild imagination. That never happened to her, she is just telling a story. She has been looking at too much television. She sees all that stuff on television." Grandmother replied, "Why did you let her watch programs like that?" He said, "you cannot monitor everything that they watch." Grandmother said, " Oh no son this child told her story too candid to have watched this on television and you need to check this story out."

However, to grandmother's knowledge, her dad let the story drop and never did anything about it. One day CPS came unexpectedly and removed Candy from the home temporarily. The father and mother became very angry with the grandmother. Candy's father phoned the grandmother to inform her it would be a long time before he talked to her again.

Candy would not see her grandmother, she was not allowed to visit her or talk with her by phone. In an effort to see Candy, grandmother arranged to visit her at school so she could at least spend some time with Candy.

Just before the Christmas party at school Candy's mother decided to take the child out of school and leave the state of Texas. Grandmother arrived at the school on the day of the Christmas party, only to find Candy would not be there. Her mother had taken her out of school earlier and she would not be back. Grandmother was so saddened by the news but she kept praying and believing God to take care of this problem.

Not only did Candy's mother not tell her grandmother, but her father was also uninformed of Candy's departure. The broken hearted, lonely father finally picked up the phone and called Candy's grandmother. This was the beginning of mending the relationship between grandmother and her son.

Praise report from Grandmother

"What happens when women pray?" I am happy to report that Candy and her mother returned home within the year. I have had the opportunity to visit with my precious Candy. She has spent the weekend with me, in my home. I am ministering (Sozo) a Greek word meaning salvation, healing, and deliverance to Candy. PRAISE THE LORD, God's word will not return to him void (Isaiah 11:12) I believe our God is turning this devastating tragedy into triumph.

SO DON"T GIVE UP BEFORE YOU RECEIVE YOUR MIRACLE!!!!!!!

February 2003- Candy gave her heart to Jesus! She was water baptized and baptized in the Holy Spirit with the evidence of speaking in tongues. Hallelujah!

TESTIMONY OF MY LIFE

Thus speaks the Lord God of Israel, saying: Write in a book for yourself all the words that I have spoken to you." (Jeremiah 30:2 NKJV)

All men are farmers, they plant their seed. The fathers are the ones who stay around for the harvest. The Bible says, *"The kingdom of heaven is likened unto a man which sowed good seed in his field: But while men slept, his enemy came and sowed tares among the wheat, and went his way. But when the blade was sprung up, and brought forth fruit, then appeared the tares also. So the servants of the householder came and said unto him Sir, didst not thou sow good seed in thy field? From whence then its tares? He said unto them, an enemy hath done this. The servants said unto him, Wilt thou then that we go and gather them up? But he said, Nay: lest while ye gather up the tares, ye root up also the wheat with them Let both grow together until the harvest: and in the time of harvest I will say to the reapers, Gather ye together first the tares, and bind them in bundles to bum them: but gather the wheat into by barn. (Matthew 13:24-30 KJV)*

The parable in Matthew 13:24-30 reminds me of what happened to me as a young child. I was an innocent five-year old child with loving parents and being a protected child so my parents thought, I knew nothing about sex. My parents did not teach me anything about sex. I suppose they did not know how to teach and discuss the issue. Silence was the way for them and many parents, as we know today during that time. If no questions were asked about sex, apparently, my parents thought there was no need to discuss the subject. When a baby was born into our family, my parents told us the stork brought the baby. However today children know better, this was not the truth, we did not question adults. Children are curious and they have thoughts, questions, and inhibitions about sex and reproduction. I know now that it was the Holy Spirit that taught me and kept me from total disaster.

One smothering, hot summer day, my three cousins came loping, like wild dogs, across the field for an extended visit at our home. That first day was the beginning of Hell for me. Our peaceful family existence was totally disrupted. Our lives would never be the same.

My relatives, all boys, were older than I. They began to teach me things about my body, their bodies, and sexual intercourse, painful and scary things that I had never known or discussed with my parents. I tried to tell my mother and father what was happening, but because they could not understand that a horrible act was being committed to me in our home, they did not listen. Also, because the perpetrators were relatives, and the boys denied the charges, my parents were in total denial. This was so painful. The feelings of abandonment and loneliness consumed me. I had no one to turn to but my parents and they were not listening. I was devastated. (*"When my father and mother forsake me, then the Lord will take care of me." Psalm 27:10 NKJV*)

At night when my parents were asleep or when they were away from home, I was always molested. I cannot remember the first time I was introduced to sexual intercourse, but I do remember those painful incidents lasting from the time I was five years old until I was eleven. I also remember the many times I tried to get help from mom and dad, and they did nothing to help me. My relatives always seemed to know when I asked for help and was refused, so the conditions of my sexual abuse continually got worse. One after the other, each boy would take my body for his own personal sexual gratification. Nothing I could say or do would make a difference. Frequently, with each boy taking his "turn" the rape sessions became so long and painful. Fighting, begging, crying, all that I did to get them to stop was in vain. Consequently, the overall feelings that I had at the time were of mistrust, fear loneliness, abandonment, and loss of self-esteem and loss of parental concern and control. I now see this abuse as the enemy coming in and sowing his tares among the wheat.

"Jesus is strong enough to defeat devils, yet gentle enough to lay His mighty hand upon you and heal your broken heart." Pastor Rod Parsley.

I learned to turn my emotions and feelings off; therefore, I would not feel anything. This time the pain was similar to an out of the body experience. It wasn't until later in life, that I learned how the sexual abuse affected me. As a wife, I would have a very difficult time reaching a climax with my husband. Many times I could not reach that ecstasy.

I feel there are millions of children who are victims of abuse. Some parents are not as protective as they should be. Although my dad is now deceased, I never had the opportunity to talk with him again about the abuse I suffered as a child. After trying many, many times, and after I became older, I finally stopped trying to talk with him about my childhood.

My mother is still living, and I have had conversations with her concerning the past sexual abuse issues. She is extremely sorry' that she was not protective of me when I needed help. In that time period many women "obeyed" their husband by conforming to what the man said. I remember that Mom never made any "major" decisions. She explained that although my dad thought he was being protective, looking back she realized he was not. As we discussed what happened, we cried together. The relationship between my mother and me took a wonderful positive turn. Even though my father has been deceased for many years, I forgave my parents for not protecting me. For years now, the relationship with my mother has been, and continues to be strong. THANK GOD, I was finally able to forgive my parents for not protecting me as a child.

"Those who created the pain of yesterday do not control the pleasure of tomorrow." Dr. Mike Murdock

Some may wonder why I would write this testimony at this time. The answer is easy to understand. Dr. Mike Murdock states: "The broken become masters at mending." It is my desire to help sexually abuse children as well as adults that have not dealt with their abuse situation. Knowing, that as children if deliverance does not take place, shame, guilt, and anger follows into adulthood. As a part of this answer, it is imperative to inform parents of how important it is to protect your children from destruction. As you are reading these pages, and you have been involved with sexual abuse or if you know someone who has been abused, deliverance is necessary. Your freedom will only come through a personal relationship with Jesus Christ. First you must receive Jesus Christ as your personal Savior. Second, you must pray and obey His teaching. Third, find a ministry or counselor that will lead you in the process of deliverance.

"O Lord my God, I cried out to You, and You healed me. Lord, You brought my soul up from the grave; You have kept me alive, that I should not go down to the pit." Psalm 30:2-3

The questions are: Why do so many children become homosexuals, lesbians, bisexual, or pregnant teens? Why are so many children promiscuous? It is because of a spirit that is transferred through behavior such as sexual abuse. The spirit is a curse from Satan. That evil spirit must be broken and destroyed. If not, it will be passed down from generation to generation until someone breaks the evil power of Satan by using the power of the Holy Spirit and the Blood of Jesus.

Parents need to know who their children are spending time with, and what they are doing. Parents should not allow their children to spend the night or to play with anyone whose background is not known. Parents cannot trust other people simply because they are neighbors, or that the children attend the same school, or attend the same church. Parents must know the moral values of other parents, if their children are involved with them.

It is proven by statistics that many children have been sexually molested by cousins, uncles, aunts, brothers, neighbors, grandparents and even their own mothers and fathers, ministers, scout leaders, church members, and other trusted adults have been known to molest children whose parents trust them with their children. Sexual abuse does not "just happen" and is then forgotten. Sexual abuse is evil. Sexual abuse scars are continuously remembered as being painful, most often over powering other tragedies, and taken to the grave unless the abused person is DELIVERED and

CLEANSED by the Blood of Jesus and filled with the Holy Spirit.

Fortunately, when the molestation finally stopped in my young life, I did not have sex or want to participate in sex again. As time passed, a miracle happened; my hymen grew back just as if I had never been violated. WHAT A MIRACLE! But the darkness still hovered over my life. I had not been totally delivered and healed. The spirit of molestation had not been destroyed.

College finally became a reality, and I was excited! Oh, was I excited, and as a college freshman, I met a young man a college senior that I thought was nice, and respectful. He asked me out on a date. I dressed up in some of my finest clothes and was excited about our date. Oh, was I surprised! This young man I thought was so respectful and nice, tried his best to rape me. Thanks be to God he was unsuccessful, and I never went out with him again.

THE HEALING PROCESS

Soon after that experience, during my college freshman days, I began to date an older freshman. We were both in the same evening class, and I thought, "A littler older man would be wiser and more thoughtful." One evening after class he took me to the same area approximately ten miles in the country where I had lived as a child, the same area where I had been molested. Being back in that area, I felt the same evil spirits I knew so well as a child. I became weak and vulnerable. My emotions were fragile, and my date knew how to control the situation. Again, I felt used and violated, as he was able to penetrate me. Shortly after this incident my boyfriend left town and the relationship ended. Later I was to learn that he was married all the time and had lied to me about this too. Once again I felt used and violated. There was a feeling of guilt and shame.

Forty years later, after I moved back to my hometown he contacted me again! This meeting was one I never thought I would experience. Since our college days, he said he had become a Christian. He apologized for his actions, the pain he had caused, and he wanted to "make things right." Although I had already forgiven him, I needed to hear him ask my forgiveness, and he needed to hear me say, "You are forgiven." This was an important part of the healing process that I had not received before. Thank God for His ability to heal and set us free. If you are violated, you may never see your perpetrator again, but you must forgive and release them. Thus: "When you change your focus you will change your feeling." Dr Mike Murdock.

Two years after my boyfriend and I ended our college relationship, I met and married my husband. However, neither my husband nor I were able to correctly address the pain and resentment of my past. Therefore, our marriage relationship had many unresolved issues, and our marriage ended after three children and twelve years of dysfunctional behavior.

Paul E Bellheimer in his book, "Don't Waste Your Sorrows" states that yielding to self-pity, depression, and rebellion is a waste of sorrow. Those who have unsuccessfully sought healing and who submit to resentment, discontent, impatience, and bitterness against God (and, may I add others) are wasting what God intended for growth in love and thus for enhanced rank in the eternal Kingdom." Thank God, He did not allow me to waste my sorrow.

Writing this book, hearing the testimonies of others, and giving my own testimony is a blessing for me. The Blood of Jesus brings healing and closure to open wounds, wounds that would otherwise hinder our personal relationship with Jesus Christ. Also, The Holy Spirit guides our ability to love and marry the Godly person as God intended. A stable relationship may never develop if one is not totally healed.

Consequently, we must know what to do to prevent the enemy from destroying our family, our nation, and our world.

In this book, I have attempted to present the truth in a practical manner. In doing so, it is my sincere desire that everyone may receive help, inspiration, and courage in an effort to prevent all others from becoming enslaved by erroneous ideas. My purpose is to better educate all who are involved with raising children to be more informed. (Yes, But How?) In today's world confusion, separation, divorce, and compromise is on a rampage. It is time to get to the ROOT of this problem: What is causing so many broken homes? The soaring divorce rate? Cohabitations? AIDS? Children born out of wedlock? The Bible states *"The night is nearly over:*

the day is almost here" (Romans 13:12 NIV) Once the cause of the problem is identified; DISOBEDIENCE and SIN (missing the mark), the road to recovery' is near. Jesus Christ is coming soon! You need to be ready.

T.D. Jakes in his book "The Lady, Her Lover and Her Lord" says "Look down at your feet and wonder what they would say if they could speak. Where have they been and from where have they run? These are the feet of America's children grown larger, but still aching. In fact, all over the world there is a mob of hurting people whose feet have run through fire rushing back home. They have tried to numb the pain through sin and did not win the peace they sought. Now since they have not been able to cry their pain to sleep, they run to Him. So, run, little feet. The Father awaits you."

The Bible's answer is to live a life that is holy and sanctified in His eyes. "But everything exposed by the LIGHT becomes visible for it is LIGHT that makes everything visible. This is why it is said, *"Wake up old sleeper! Rise from the dead and Christ will shine upon you." (Ephesians* 5:12-14) The Holy Spirit will shine in the homes of all people that begin to seek God and his ways. Therefore, allow Jesus Christ to come into your life.

These anointed words of wisdom and personal knowledge were written expressly and purposefully to deliver us from the evil one. May the God of Glory sanctify you, cleanse you, and make you complete, whole and ready to meet Jesus Christ. Amen.

Let God's Word be your guide. Jesus Christ is the only answer for the world today. He is able to keep that which is committed to him against this very day.

Have you placed your children in the hands of Jesus Christ? If you have not, I challenge you to do so now-without delay, because Jesus Christ is coming soon. As that day approaches, the pressures of evil are bearing down on the family structure with great force. IF YOU AND YOUR FAMILY ARE NOT COMMITED TO JESUS CHRIST, YOU ARE IN GRAVE DANGER OF HELL'S FIRES! WILL YOU AND YOUR FAMILY SURVIVE THE RAGING STORMS OF LIFE?

The Bible say's *"Brother will betray brother to death, and a father his child; children will rebel against their parents and have them put to death. All men will hate you because of me, BUT HE WHO STANDS FIRM TO THE END WILL BE SAVED. (Matthew 10:21-22 also Micah 7:6-7)*

20 Questions Interview-By: Alva Wilson

QUESTIONS FOR THE PARENT OF A SEXUAL ABUSE VICTIM

1). Did you have any idea your child was being molested? If not, when and how did you find out?

Answer: I had no idea whatsoever that my child was being molested. I found out by way of another parent whose child had been molested by this person and they were trying to warn me regarding what type of person this man was and to advise me to keep my child away from him. Unfortunately, when this woman told me, it was already too late. When I finally worked through all the various stages of emotions after I realized that this possibility of molestation was more than likely a reality, I had to plan how to confront my child. What I did was to take my child to a place I felt was peaceful and serene, and told my child I had some questions to ask, but that I first needed to inform him I had decided I would no longer allow him to have anything whatsoever to do with this man, and that he would not be allowed to see this man again. This was done so that my child would not hesitate to be totally honest with me. I felt like my child might be afraid that this man might be taken away from him along with all the individual attention and all that goes with it, if he confessed what was going on. By eliminating the possibility of ever seeing this man again, gave my child nothing to loose by telling the truth. After much probing and careful questioning, everything finally came out. Every filthy detail.

2). How did you feel when you found out?

Answer: I guess first of all, I was in denial. This couldn't be happening to my child. Then I was outraged and the possibility of this happening, particularly since it was happening in a religious organizational program. But then I remembered, when I confronted God about what was happening (actually, I was accusing God), that is when I first met this man, my first thought regarding him was something along the lines of "yuck," this guy is really creepy; I sure hope he isn't some kind of pervert or something. The reality is that God, by His Holy Spirit, whom, as a baby Christian, I had not come to really know or sense yet, had warned me about this man's character. Had I yielded to my first impression of this person, I don't believe any of the horrible things that happened, would have taken place. I was pretty much hysterical and didn't know what to do so I informed a very close friend and asked for help. This friend, who loved us dearly, but who was not a Christian, told me he would make some calls and have this guy taken care of. He wanted this man's address and description. Well, as much as I wanted this man to suffer the worse agony imaginable, I knew I would have to answer to God if I gave my friend any of the information requested. I did however, get a shotgun, and put it in my closet, just in case.

3). Did you blame yourself?

Answer: Yes, in many ways I still do. I know that I have been forgiven for missing God's voice in all of this, but I also know I was in a somewhat shaky place spiritually at the time which left doors open for the enemy to sneak in, which he did like gang busten. I did not go with my gut feeling which I now know was the Holy Spirit's voice, and I was not aware of the great need in my child's heart for a friend, or father figure. Being a single parent, I had allowed myself to be deceived into thinking I could be all that my children needed a mother, and a father figure. I blame myself for not seeing that void and also for not stopping to take the time to try to fill it. I was too involved with my own life. Thus when the enemy put a substitute in the life of my child, to give my child love, attention, and affection; my child grabbed it with both arms not realizing it was a deadly trap.

4). Did you feel guilty?

Answer: Honestly, I did allow the enemy to smack me with guilt much more often than I should. When something as devastating as child molestation happens to a little one, it almost always leaves deeply -embedded scars in the life of that child (and in fact the whole family generally). When I see my child suffering or going through trials that I know are a direct result of this diabolical thing that happened to him as a child, I have to really fight to deflect the pangs of guilt that hit me.

5). Did you feel that there was something you could have done to prevent the molestation?

Answer: Again, if I had been more vigilant over my child's heart, soul, and even body; and had kept the lines of communication open and been able to test the emotional atmosphere or the heart, I may have seen a problem. If I had known to hear and follow the leading of God's Spirit that would have definitely stopped this catastrophe. If I had really checked into the nature and character of this person more, for myself before I allowed my child to spend time with him and then monitored their times together by gentle communication with my child, maybe I could have prevented this disaster. But, I didn't; and all of the 'would have' and the 'could haves' in the world don't make a bit of difference at all. My desire is that maybe this will help to instruct other parents to be mindful of questionable signs they see in their child, and possible areas where their relationships with their child has grown weak.

6). Do you feel that you had been as watchful as you could have possibly been?

Answer: I know that I have always dearly loved my children and have been extremely concerned regarding their welfare (even though I may not have always shown it). I guess the one thing that really comes to mind when I consider this question is that we, in general, NEVER THINK THIS KIND OF HORRIBLE STUFF CAN HAPPEN TO US. I did, in the natural, all I knew to do regarding my child's welfare in this situation. I DID ask the assistant pastor about this man and he gave a good report regarding the makeup. I saw this man being kind to my child, to some degree, basking in the attention he was getting from this man. I saw NO SIGNS, at least none that I recognized, that there was any problem whatsoever. The truth of it is, when I found out, I was in agony that my child hadn't known or trusted me enough to be able to tell me what was happening. Rather, my child believed the threats of this man, that if my child told anyone, he would hurt my child and his mommy. Knowing that your child doesn't have the confidence in you to be able to feel assured that you are a place of sure safety, and a place where no one can come and hurt them, or their home or anything else dear to them, is so crushing.

7). *Did you know and trust the person who was the perpetrator?*

Answer: I knew only what I was told. This man 'acted' caring and interested in my child's welfare. He lavished interest and attention in everything my child did and said. I had this man over to our home for dinner and to visit in an effort to get to know him better. He had had a shining reference by someone I trusted as to his love and interest in children. Because there was no father figure in my home, I had been trying to find someone who could bring that image of Godly fatherhood and manhood into my home as an example to my children. I believed what I was told about this man and opened our home and our hearts to him.

8). *Were you afraid to confront him or her?*

Answer: Along with extreme anger at what this man had

done, there came a dreaded fear of him. I guess my thought was that anyone who could be so diabolical, as to do such dreadful things to children must be evil personified. So, my desire to punish him was mixed with an unreasonable fear of him. Thus, the shot gun in my closet, as mentioned above.

9). *How did you handle this fear of confrontation?*

Answer: At first this situation messed me up so bad that I actually got into bed and covered my head, vowing never to come out again. I was devastated. I wouldn't let my children go near the doors or windows and I live in sheer terror for a few days. Then one afternoon, I guess I saw what could be called a vision. I saw Satan standing in the corner of my room laughing at me as if to say 'Gotcha'! Well, this made me so mad, I got up out of bed and said, 'Oh no you don't'. It was then that I started to take steps toward having this man dealt with.

10). *Looking back on how you handled it, do you feel as though you should have handled it differently?*

Answer: Due to the fact that I was very much in a state of shock during several weeks after finding out about this man molesting my child, I know that my reactions were slow and limited. I was without financial resources to do what I would have really like to do, which was send this man away for life (it was later found out that he had molested several other boys and had in fact been incarcerated for doing so). I was only able to secure the public defender's office as my resource. I also did not have any way of knowing or coping with the emotional side of the situation. I probably was not as supportive to my child, nor knowledgeable with regards to what needed to be done to help my child as I could have; had I known what all to do. It took several years, even with counseling, before my child was able to function somewhat normally in school situations. Please know, that situations such as this will indeed, FOREVER, change the life of a child and need to be handled with all the skill and resources possible with the direction of God.

11). *Did your feelings for your child change? If so, how did they change? Did they change for the better or did your relationship get worse?*

Answer: I guess my initial feelings were that I just did not understand. I hadn't seen the great need that my child was feeling. And I guess to be honest, I just didn't understand how this dreadful man could have seduced my child's mind like he did. My child was a bright, caring child who I thought was close to me. I couldn't understand how my child bad been lied to regarding the rightness of what this man was doing, and threatened about telling anyone, etc., and my child believed the lies. It made me feel like such a failure that I had failed to instruct and protect my innocent baby from such evil. I have since learned that children can be easily seduced into doing things that they would not or should not do. All it takes is the right bait. I do believe my child and I got closer after this happened. In fact, we may have gotten too close as I think we seemed to feel like 'we' were all we had; the only ones we could trust in the whole world. I became over protective to some extent, and I guess my child became a bit over dependent in some ways. I don't know if my child would agree with that. It has taken years to establish a healthier relationship.

12). *Do you feel your child blames you for what happened? If so, how does that make you feel?*

Answer: I had never really asked my child that question. I think I have always felt that my child knew I did all I could do when I found out what had happened. My biggest concern was that my child did not blame me, which was a very real problem for a long time. (This is a very common reaction for children to what has happened). I was desperate for my child to see that he was not to blame AT ALL. I was ashamed to have to admit to my child that I had failed. It is ALWAYS EXTREMELY IMPORTANT for a child to know they have a safe place and a safe person in which they can hide, but I had allowed all of this to happen so I felt I had lost that position.

13). *What advise would you give to the reader as one parent to another to help them prevent such a situation from happening?*

Answer: ALWAYS, always, monitor your child's activities, emotions, moods, words, and attitudes. ALWAYS, keep open the doors of communication. Sit down EVERYDAY and talk with your child. More importantly, listen to your child. And don't pooh-pooh ANYTHING that they say. Listen to, consider, do whatever it takes to cover and protect your child. Never give up that place of safety for them. And always remember that a child is a gift from God and that his life should be first priority to every parent. The parent's needs must always come second to a child's.

14). *What advice would you give to help a broken, hurting child once he or she had been molested?*

Answer: Find someone who will listen. Look and tell everyone you trust until someone does something to help you. There are people who care and want to help.

15). *What advice would you give to children to assist them in preventing sexual molestation?*

Answer: Never keep ANY SECRETS. If someone tells YOU not to tell your parents something, run away from them as fast as you can and TELL YOUR PARENTS right away. Never let ANYONE, touch you or talk to you in a way that makes you feel uncomfortable or goes against what you have been taught is right and good, no matter what that person tells you. If you don't feel totally good about what is said to you deep inside you, run away and tell someone right away.

16). What advice, if any, would YOU give a potential molester or pedophile?

Answer: I would tell them that they need Jesus. <u>**I do NOT believe under any circumstances that a child molester can be changed any way other than by surrendering their life to the Lord Jesus Christ!**</u>. I believe that pedophilia is a demonic influence and all the medication and therapy in the world will not make that influence go away. <u>A molester may be able to "act right" for a while, but they are still a molester and will definitely molest again given the right circumstances.</u> If they aren't given the circumstances, they will make their own circumstances. I believe this can be verified by checking the records of any pedophiles.

17). Do you think it is possible to remain friendly and helpful to someone that has hurt your child and you?

Answer: I don't see how this can really be done. As a Christian, I'm expected to love my enemy. I realize that many molesters have been themselves molested and should to some degree be pitied. However, I believe that befriending the person who violated your child is betrayal to that child. Think about it, how can you be considered a 'safe place' if you have invited the person who has so damaged your child's life, into that place of safety? What must your child think of this, that your friendship (or marriage) is more important than his or her safety? And how can a child be at peace having to see this person regularly, not to mention having to worry about it happening again? Run as fast as you can from the offender and slam and bolt the door.

18). Do you feel there is help for the victim of sexual abuse? And if so, what should they do?

Answer: Again, Jesus is the only real and true deliverance from the wounds and scars of sexual abuse. Medication and therapy is merely a band aid to cover a much deeper wound. Until those deep hurts and scars are cleansed, ministered to, and healed, there will always be turmoil and problems in the life of an abused person.

19). Do you feel there is help for a molester or pedophile? If so, what should they do?

Answer: Please see the answer to question #16.

20). What is the best way to deal with your child after you find out he or she has been the victim of sexual abuse?

Answer: Unconditional love, support and acceptance. This is a baby who has been lied to, victimized, and violated. Be available to talk or be quiet, as the child needs. Be unjudgemental of that child, regardless of how YOU might feel inside. Be supportive and understanding of what he or she has to say. Believe what he or she says and always reassure the child.

Yes, But How?

How Do I Get Free??

FORGIVENESS IS ESSENTIAL
   FORGIVE
   ✓ Fear is your worst enemy
   ✓ Overcome it today
   ✓ Rise to greater heights
   ✓ God has already made the way
   ✓ Intervened by his grace and mercy
   ✓ Victory is yours, I say
   ✓ Eternally

KNOW THAT God wants you free. Forgiveness is essential. By Alva Wilson

YOU shall know the truth and the truth shall make you free.

A WORD OF ENCOURAGEMENT TO THE SEXUALLY ABUSED VICTIM

I will emphasize again it is not your fault. The guilt you are experiencing or have felt in times past belongs to your sex offender. It does not belong to you. Nevertheless, you must release you family member(s) forgive your parents or the responsible adult that did not protect you, forgive the perpetrator and forgive yourself. STOP BLAMING YOURSELF.

Only believe that God is able to heal and deliver you. The healing process will begin when you forgive. You were a victim, but now you are a survivor who has overcome by faith. I call you a Victor.

You may feel that your slate has been wiped clean. However you can never get away from your past. It keeps haunting you. LET IT GO!

World renound Gospel singer Sandy Patty gave testimony of her past abusive life. She states that, *"Wounded people attract wounded people. "*

It is absolutely astounding how your past life effects your present life and the future decisions that you make. Those sins in your life must be confronted by you and dealt with, or they will surface again in your life when you least expect them to do so.

Sandy Patty's first marriage was destroyed after several years with her husband and children. She says the sexual abuse inflicted upon her as a child was never confronted. A trusted friend of the family sexually abused her; a woman teacher that her parents never suspected was abusing her. Sandy says that the abuse affected her marriage. Statistics prove that the sexually abused woman or man that has not been healed will have severe problems in marriage. Many end in divorce-just as Sandy's did. She was broken and left fragmented. Neither the sexual abuse nor the abuser was ever confronted. Sandy never told her parents or anyone. Therefore she was not healed before entering into a marriage relationship, as is the case with so many people. They often wonder what is wrong in their marriage.

Never realizing the devastating effect sexual abuse has on one's marriage relationship (if not confronted and dealt with), will cause major problems. Do you remember "The Little House on the Prairie?" This was a television series from the 70's in which Alison Arngrim starred. She recently revealed (On Larry King Live, CNN) her deep dark secret after 27 years of marriage and silence. She stated that from ages 6-9 years of age, she was sexually abused by a relative.

Please do not let fear keep you bound up and afraid to tell a trusted adult. The deep, dark secret must be exposed. It has been haunting you too long. The sexual abuse may have happened 40 or 50 years ago, but you must get help to get healed.
" And forgive. ..

Parents Please Listen

The ugly secret and shame of child molestation is usually carried over into the adult years. From the time of molestation until the person is able to break their "silence of shame," they suffer alone as they are afraid to speak of the terrible molestation just as the perpetrator directed. Other signs of sexual abuse in children, toddlers, preschool, school age children and teenagers are: nightmares, withdrawal, violent play, low self-esteem, afraid to undress, running away from home, unprovoked crying spells, outburst of anger, early sexual promiscuity, fear of being alone, vaginal discharge, unusual odor in genital area, fear of pregnancy or pregnancy. Some refuse to go to school or they would leave school early, fear of a certain person, situation or stranger, pain, itching, bleeding, bruises or problems walking or sitting. Some experience behavior problems at school and a change in school performance.

These children suffer alone because they are afraid to speak of the terrible molestation just as the perpetrator directed. The molestation and the threat for silence bring self blame, shame, fear and all these continuously press on the conscious until the victim becomes illogical and then, in many cases, the victim becomes the victimizer. Statistics show that most victims wait to discuss their dark secret of molestation for an average of 21 years, and an average of 120 children are molested before that one pedophile is caught.

The National Center on Child Abuse and Neglect in Washington, DC estimates that every year in the United States more than 60,000 children are sexually abused; 100,000 children are physically abused, and over 1,000 die from abuse and neglect from caregivers. Furthermore, the top three vocations of sexual predators are employed in the Church, in teaching positions or youth workers.

As safety precautions, children should be taught many things including simple facts such as:
- A parent or trusted adult take children to a public restroom;
- Children know that their bodies are private and no one has permission to touch them;
- Gifts, candy, and secrets do not give anyone permission to seduce;
- Say "NO" and tell a trusted adult;
- Internet port sites lure potential victims

On a positive note, many child oriented organizations are

currently implementing adult worker screening plans, having youth workers in teams of two or more, and many organizations have banned sleep-over type events.

A WORD TO THE SEX OFFENDER

A great man of God, Leonard Ravenhill once said, "It' s not too late for mercy yet I don't care how twisted and corrupt your life is at this moment-is not too late to ask for forgiveness," and might I add counseling, prayer, and deliverance. "God can and will forgive you if you will repent of your sin, plead the blood of Christ and ask for mercy! It is not too late to ask for mercy." You wonder, "Can God really forgive all the rottenness and corruption in my life?" He certainly can. Why? Because today Jesus is still on the throne of mercy. You can find grace and His help. However, when we see Him at the Judgment, He will no longer be seated on the throne of mercy. He will be seated on the throne of justice. His first time on earth, He was a tender Christ, the Lamb of God, who went about kissing little babies and blessing people. There is nothing more beautiful than a little lamb, but there is nothing more terrible than the wrath of The Lamb.

"Shall not the judge of all the earth do right?" (Gen.18:25) If a man or woman is torn with lust, if his mind is full of wickedness, if by his own actions he ask to be cast away from God with his own misery forever and ever-then what? God shall bring every work into judgment with every secret thing.

Accept the love, mercy and forgiveness of Christ. Joe R. Barnett says it this way: "People in Jesus' Day couldn't understand why he wasted his time associating with failures. He did it because he knew they could turn from failure to success if they were properly motivated. And this method of motivation was to love them, forgive them, and believe in them

They weren't accustomed to that kind of treatment. And it worked. They responded to it.

Remember Zacchaeus? He was a hated tax collector. He had made a mess of his life. Everyone knew that. One day Jesus said,

"Come on Zacchaeus, I'm going home with you." Because Jesus believed in this little man, he changed. He said, "Lord I'm going to give half my income to take care of the poor, and anyone I've cheated I'm going to repay four times the amount.

Just as Jesus went to Zacchaeus' house, He wants to come visit your house too! Invite Him in. He loves you despite your bazaar behavior-but He hates the sin in your life, what you are doing or have done to others. Jesus wants to make you free from the pain of your past. Will you invite him in? Whom the Son sets free is free indeed. **REPENT!...**

A WORD ON GENERATIONAL CURSES

David had already sinned against God as is recorded in 2 Samuel 12:9 "Wherefore has thou despised the commandment of the Lord, to do evil in his sight? Thou has killed Uriah the Hittite with the sword, and has taken his wife to be thy wife, and has slain him with the sword of the children of Ammon.

Now therefore the sword shall never depart from thine house; because thou hast despised me, and hast taken the wife of Uriah, the Hittite to be thy wife. Behold, I will raise up evil against thee out of thine own house, and I will take thy wives before thine eyes, and give them unto thy neighbor, ... Thus saith the Lord.

In verse 13, David's next Chapter, II Samuel 12, David's heartaches began. In many instances when a man or woman commit adultery, fornication or any sexual sin, Satan lies to them and they believe him. "Oh, go ahead, this is just between you and me; nobody else will hurt by what we do." What a lie!

Oh my brother, oh my sister, take a good look at what happened in David's family. David's sin opened the door for rape and incest to begin between his son and daughter. After that came murder. Think about it! "The sword shall never depart from thine house" saith the Lord.

Shortly after David had committed adultery with Bathsheba, his daughter Tamar's life was ruined by her own brother. David had a son named Absolom. Tamar, his sister, was very pretty. Amnon was also the son of David by another wife. Amnon loved Tamar. He loved her so much that he became sick (love sick). He thought it would be very hard for him to do anything to her. However, Amnon had a friend that he confided in. He was a very subtle man. Therefore, he told Amnon how to have sex with his own sister. Lie down on your bed and pretend to be very ill; and when your father, King David comes to see you, ask him to let your sister Tamar come and give you food that you may see her prepare it, and let her feed you. When David came to visit Amnon, he gave the King his request. It was granted. So, Tamar went to Amnon's house. He was lying in bed. She prepared his food but he refused to eat it.

He then ordered all the men servants to leave him alone. So, they did. Amnon said to Tamar, bring my food into my bedroom, so you can feed me. Tamar took the food which she had prepared and brought it into his bedroom. When she came into his bedroom to feed him, he took hold of her and forced her to come lye with him. She yelled no! You are my brother. Do not force me. You should not do this in Israel. Please do not do this foolish thing. This is so shameful for me. Where will I go? And as for you Amnon, you will be looked upon as one of the fools in Israel. Now ask your father, King David, if he will allow you to marry me. He will not withhold me from you. However, Amnon would not listen to her, but being stronger than she, forced her and lay (raped) with her.

Consequently, Amnon hated her accordingly. His hatred for her was greater than the love he had for her before the rape. Then he put her out. He called his servants and said, "put this woman out of here and halt the door behind her." In shame and sadness, Tamar put ashes on her head, tore her beautiful dress of many colors that she had on, laid her hand on her head and left there crying. How said! Her father, King David's sin caused all this trauma – a generational curse. Now comes more consequences. Tamar told her other brothers Ahsalom. He was so hurt and angry that he decided to kill Amnon. So, he devised a scheme to get his brother out into a battle and kill him. (II Samuel 13:22; 28)

Now Absolom had commanded his servants to watch Amnon when his heart is merry with wine. Kill him, when I give your orders. Don't be afraid to smite him and kill him. So they did by appointment of Absolom. Absolom had determined from the day that Amnon forced his sister, Tamar, that he would kill him.

These generational curses came upon David and his children, because of his own sexual immorality. It is so important that you watch yourself, do not commit any kind of sin, especially sexual sins. It hurt generations to come, long after you are dead and gone. Sexual molestation is a generational curse. The good news is "It can be broken." I challenge you to make a decision to break all curses now. Set you, your family, and loved ones free! Use the name of Jesus, apply the blood of the Lamb and command Satan to release those trapped in his bondage. Set the captives free.

EPILOGUE ONE: POEMS
POEMS CHILDREN LEARN
WHAT THEY LIVE

If a child lives with criticism
He learns to condemn.
If a child lives with hostility, He learns to fight.
If a child lives with ridicule, He learns to be shy.
If a child lives with jealousy, He learns to feel guilty.
If a child lives with tolerance, He learns to be patient.
If a child lives with encouragement, He learns to be confident.
If a child lives with praise, He learns to appreciate.
If a child lives with fairness, He learns justice.
If a child lives with security, He learns to have faith.
If a child lives with approval, He learns to like himself.
If a child lives with acceptance and friendship,
He learns to find life in the world.

Dorothy Law Nolte

Walk a Little Plainer Daddy

Walk a little plainer daddy
Said a little boy so frail
I'm following in your footsteps
And I don't want to fail
Sometimes they are hard to see
So walk a little plainer daddy
For you are leading me.
I know that once you walked this way
Many years ago
And what you did along the way
I'd really like to know
For sometimes when I am tempted
I don't know what to do
So walk a litter plainer daddy
For I must follow you.

Someday when I've, grown up
You are like I want to be
Then I will have a little boy
Who will want to follow me
And I would want to lead him right
And help him to be true
So walk a little plainer daddy
For we must follow you.
Author unknown

Misty

My name is Misty, I am but three.
My eyes are swollen, I cannot see.
I must have been bad,
That lesson I've learned. For I am punished
With cigarette burns.
I have to be right.
I cannot be wrong.
For I am locked up all week long.

When I wake up,
I'm all alone.
The house is dark.
My parents aren't home.
Deep inside I feel so bad.
For I am hated by my Mom and Dad.
I'm just an expensive joke.
They need money for speed and coke!
An accident, yes.
That is their word.
Countless times,
That phrase I've heard.
Another burn,
I cannot endure.
They see me as a lot of trouble,
I am sure.
Be quiet now!
I hear a car.
My dad is home,
From Charlie's Bar.
I hear his cuss.
My name he calls.
I squeeze against
The dirty walls,
O, Dear God,
It is too late.
His face is turning to hate.
I feel the pain again and again.
Oh, please Lord let it end.
My name was Misty.
I was but three.
For last night,
My father murdered me.

Don't pick up that belt
Or extension cord, please.
I'll do anything,

I'll kneel on my knees
For hours or days
Whatever you say.
But please don't beat me,
At least not today.
For today should be new
A new start, you see,
Where you know I love you
And you show you love me
Not with anger or pain,
But in positive ways.
For the bruises will heal,
But the pain in me stays.

Author Unknown

PROMISES, PR0MISES

(A child's view of incest),

I asked for your help
and you told me you would,
if I told you the things
my dad did to me
It was really hard for me
to say all those things,
but you told me to trust you
then you made me repeat them
to fourteen different strangers.

I asked you for privacy and you sent
two policemen to my school,
in front of everyone,
like I was the one being busted.

I asked you to believe me,
And you said that you did.
Then you connected me to a lie detector
and took me to court where lawyers
put me on trial like I was a liar.

I asked you for help
and you gave me a doctor
with cold metal gadget and cold hands
who spread my legs and stared,
just like my father.

I asked you for confidentiality
and you let the newspaper
get my story.

I asked for protection and
you gave me a social worker
who patted my head
and called me Honey.
She sent me to live with strangers
in another place, with a different school

I asked for help and forced my Mom
to choose between us
she was scared and had a lot to lose.
I had a lot to lose too;
The difference was that
you never told me how much.

I asked you to put an end to the abuse.
You put an end to my whole family.
You took away my nights of hell
And gave me days of hell instead.
You've exchanged my private nightmare
for a very public one.
(Author Unknown)

IF I HAD MY CHILD TO RAISE AGAIN

If I had my child to raise over again,
I'd build self-esteem first, and the house later.
I'd finger-paint more, and point the finger less.
I would do less correcting and more connecting.
I'd take my eyes off my watch, and watch with my eyes.
I would care to know less and know to care more.
I'd take more hikes and fly more kites.

I'd stop playing serious, and seriously play.
I would run through more fields and gaze at more stars.
I'd do more hugging and less tugging.
I'd see the oak tree in the acorn more.
I would be firm less often, and affirm much more.
I'd model less about the love of power,
And more about the power of love.

Author Unknown

THE STARFISH FLINGER

As the old man walked the beach
At dawn, he noticed a young man
ahead of him picking up starfish
and flinging them into the sea.
Finally catching up with the
youth, he asked him why he was doing this.
The answer was that the stranded starfish
would die if left until the morning sun.

"But the beach goes on for miles,
and there are millions of starfish"
countered the other.
"How can your effort make any difference?"

The young man looked at the starfish
in his hand and then threw it to safety
in the waves.
"It makes a difference to this one, " he said.

Minnesota Literacy Council

James Robison is a product of a 42-year-old rape victim. He is
alive and well today. He is a T.V. minister of the Gospel of Jesus
Christ. <u>One person heard his mother's cry for help</u>. A pastor's wife
answered an ad in the newspaper. She adopted James Robison and
raised him up in a Christian home. Today he is one of the greatest
Evangelists the world has ever known.

If only one person read this book and is helped, it will be worth
the time, energy and resources to publish this book.

EPILOGUE TWO: PRAYERS
PRAYERS OF REPENTANCE

(Prayer of Salvation)

Pray this prayer out loud so you can hear yourself speak. The Bible says, "With the heart man believes unto righteousness and with the MOUTH confession is made unto salvation." To believe "with the heart" is to believe with your spirit man, your inner man. "Righteousness" is your right standing in the sight of God. TO BE CONSIDERED BY GOD TO BE FAULTLESS, GUILTLESS, AND BLAMESLESS BECAUSE YOU ARE IN HIS SON, JESUS CHRIST, WHO HAS ALREADY PAID THE PENALTY FOR YOUR SALVATION. "Salvation" is wholeness, completeness, without blemish.

When you speak to your spirit (inner man) it takes hold of your words. **WHEN YOU SPEAK THE WORD OF GOD** your spirit takes hold to that Word and the Power of God begin to work in your life.

I set before you blessing and cursing, life and death, CHOOSE LIFE.

"Dear Jesus, I now realize that I am a sinner and that you died for me. I repent of my sins and iniquities and I ask that You come into my heart. Save my family and me and take us to heaven. In Jesus' Name. I thank you for Salvation. AMEN.

(Prayer of Repentance and Deliverance from Shame) By Dr. Larry Lea

"Dear Jesus, thank You for bearing all of my shame in Your body on the cross. Your Grace is sufficient! Right now, I give all my shame over to You so You can apply your death on the cross to it. I believe my shame was crucified with You on Calvary's cross and I count it as dead to me from this moment on.

I covenant with You in my own inner man, from this day forward to treat shame as a dead issue in my life. I will not hear its lying voice about others or me. I will rebuke shame openly every time it tries to resurrect its power over my life and destiny in You. I will turn to You immediately and get Your opinion every time. I will make sure it is Your voice speaking to me by hiding Your Word in my heart. I will not sin against You by mistaking the voice of shame for Your voice.

I confess every shame-producer in my life right now as sin, and I reject them from this point forward. I turn away from my shame-producing activities and thank You for helping me overcome their influence. I fully expect to over-come every obstacle to my God-given destiny that You have reserved for me. I ask You to renew my passion and love for You daily, Jesus, Your Word and Your Spirit. I commit to you now that I will persist in overcoming all shame in my life, with Your help. I praise and thank You because I know You hear me.

The Truth About The Blood

You shall know the truth and the truth {that you know) shall make you free.

Are you a believer in Jesus Christ? Do you know without a shadow of a doubt that Jesus Christ shed his blood for you almost 2000 years ago? Or have you just heard these words over and over again, yet the true sense of the meaning of Jesus' crucifixion has somehow lost its' importance in your life. Perhaps like so many others, you never knew or gave much thought to the seven places that Jesus shed his blood and was bruised for you.

The significance of this truth is virtually important and imperative for you to understand in order to be totally delivered. Thank God for Pastor Larry Huch and his book, Free At Last. This book is a "must read," for all to understand the true meaning of the Blood of Jesus in the seven places where Jesus shed his blood.

In this chapter, I will expound on the seven places where he shed his blood. This is absolutely imperative to the sexually abused. The scriptures say "that he was wounded for our transgressions, he was bruised for our iniquities; the chastisement of our peace was upon him and with his stripes, we are healed." (Isaiah 53:5). Jesus' blood delivered us from inner hurts and iniquities. His bruises won our deliverance from inner hurt and iniquities. If you have a bruise on your body, it means you are bleeding on the inside says Pastor Larry Huch. When one has been sexually abused, he or she is left with a gaping wound. That wound never closes. It is left to heal all by itself. What a tragedy. The bruise remains for a lifetime unless one is healed and delivered from its effects.

Sexual abuse is a wound that goes very deep and lasts a lifetime. The wound is left bleeding from the inside. One reason it is so hard to detect the sexual abuse victim is you cannot see the gaping wounds with natural eyesight, but it is detected through dysfunctional behavior. Sometimes years after the abuse takes place, the dysfunctional behavior continues until deliverance takes place.

Thank God for the blood of Jesus. The good news is God will heal what has been done. The wounds from within and the scars from the outside. He will restore the power inside and outside says Pastor Huch, so that you can walk in total victory.

It is absolutely essential to understand and appropriate the blood of Jesus in your prayers. The blood sets you free.

Receive Jesus Christ as Lord and Savior of Your Life

The Bible says, "That if thou shalt confess with thy mouth the Lord Jesus, and shalt believe in thine heart that God raised him from the dead, thou shalt be saved. For with the heart man believeth unto righteousness; and with the mouth confession is made unto salvation" (Romans 10:9,10).

To receive Jesus Christ as Lord and Savior of your life, sincerely pray this prayer from your heart.

Dear Jesus:

I believe that You died for me and that You rose again on the third day. I confess to You that I am a sinner and that I need Your love and forgiveness. Come into my life, forgive my sins, and give me eternal life. I confess You now as my Lord. Thank You for my salvation.

Write to us:
Alva Wilson Ministries, P.O. Box 1196, Rowlett, TX 75030-1196
We will send you information to help you with
your new life in Christ.

PRAYER REQUEST(S)

Let us join our faith with yours for your prayer needs.
Fill out the coupon below and send to:
Alva Wilson Ministries, P.O. Box 1196, Rowlett, TX 75030-1196

Prayer Request(s):

_____

_____

_____

_____

_____

_____

_____

(PLEASE PRINT)

Name:_____

Address:_____

City: _____ State:_____ Zip:_____

Phone: _____

ABOUT THE AUTHOR

Alva Wilson is a mother of three children and seven grandchildren. Her precious mother, Ann Oliver is a retired minister who accompanies Alva on some evangelistic trips, interceding on her behalf.

Alva, a native Texan, has traveled to many parts of the world; preaching and teaching the Word of God. She ministers across America as well as Mexico, England, Germany, Israel and most recently Norway and Southern England. She knows that God has equipped her to "Go ye therefore and teach all nations..."

She is a graduate of World Harvest Bible College of Columbus, Ohio; Attended Oral Roberts University. A member of World Harvest Church Ministerial Association; Ordained by Pastor Rod Parsley. Other accomplishments include Bachelor of Arts, Masters and Doctorate of Missionary Degree. She is an ordained Elder under Dr. Morris Cerullo World Evangelism (MCWE).

Many are delivered and set free by the wind and fire of the Holy Ghost and the "Breakers Annointing" that Alva brings.

NOTES

Jakes, T.D., <u>Naked and Not Ashamed</u>, Destiny Image Publishers, Inc. 1997.

Morris, Marilyn, "The Repercussions of Sex," April 2000. AIMS For Success Inc., Dallas, Texas.

Sumrall, Dr. Lester, "The World of Family," Adapted from the book, <u>Seven Steps to Taking Charge of Your Life</u>.

Drake, Elizabeth D. and Gilroy, Anne E., "Parent's Checklist For the Prevention of Child Abuse." Prevent Child Abuse Texas. Children's Trust Fund of Texas, 1986.

Huch, Larry, <u>Free At Last, Whitaker House, New Kensington, PA., 2002-2004,</u>

Powers, Marie, "Shame the Thief of Intimacy."

Sills, Judith, Ph.D., "A Woman's Guide to Loving Lasting Relationships."

Billhermer, Paul E., "Don't Waste Your Sorrows"

Prevent Child Abuse Texas

12701 Research #303
Austin, Texas 78759
512.250.8438 *tel*
512.250.8733 *fax*
pcatx@juno.com

TO: Alva Wilson

FROM: Wendell Teltow, Executive Director

RE: Permission to Use Printed Material

DATE: April 10, 2001

Please feel free to use any of our printed material regarding child abuse/prevention in your book. Please note that all material quoted needs to be referenced regarding the source (Prevent Child Abuse Texas).

Thank you,

Wendell Teltow
Executive Director
Prevent Child Abuse Texas

Prevent Child Abuse Texas
12701 Research Blvd., #303, Austin, TX 78759, 512.250.8438 *tel* 512.250.8733 *fax*
www.preventchildabusetexas.org pcatx@preventchildabusetexas.org *email*

TEXAS DEPARTMENT OF PROTECTIVE AND REGULATORY SERVICES

Date: 12/6/2001

RE:

Dear

On behalf of the Child Protective Services, I would like to thank you for taking the time to share your concerns about the above named child(ren).

Upon receiving your report, I was assigned to assess the family situation to determine the need for CPS intervention. After contacting the family, victim(s), and collateral resources, as needed, and reviewing the facts of the case with my supervisor, we have determined that the family does not require our service at this time.

Once again, thank you for your interest and concern for the family. If you have any questions or concerns, feel free to call me at (254) 750-9241 ext.

In the future, if you have reason to believe that any child is at risk of abuse/neglect, please contact the child abuse hotline or your local law enforcement.

Sincerely,

Printed in the United States
215200BV00001B/5/A